International Space Law: United Nations Instruments

UNITED NATIONS
New York, 2017

ST/SPACE/61/REV.2

Publishing production: English, Publishing and Library Section, United Nations Office at Vienna.

Foreword

International Space Law and the United Nations Office for Outer Space Affairs

The year 1967 represented a milestone in space history with the entry into force of the foundational instrument of international space law: the *Treaty on Principles Governing the Activities of States in the Exploration and Use of Outer Space, including the Moon and Other Celestial Bodies.* I am now pleased to present this latest treaty booklet, which documents this first treaty and subsequent key developments in international space law. The series of treaty booklets have been produced by the Office for more than two decades, and have proved to be a useful and comprehensive source of information for a wide range of space professionals, including law and policymakers, technical and economics specialists, as well as researchers and scholars.

The preparation of the treaty booklets has always been an integral part of the Office's broader efforts in the field of capacity-building in international space law. Since 2001, the Office has organized international workshops on capacity-building in space law, which have provided a useful platform for professionals to exchange information on space law, and on how to apply it and strengthen it. Furthermore, the Office's website contains a database of documents relating to the regulation of national space activities. The website also shows the Office's multi-year effort to develop comprehensive *travaux préparatoires* for the United Nations treaties on outer space.

Besides the above-mentioned major capacity-building efforts of the Office, its technical functions relating to international space law also deserve attention. On behalf of the Secretary-General, the Office discharges responsibilities under the United Nations treaties and principles on outer space, including the maintenance of the United Nations Register of Objects Launched into Outer Space, established in accordance with the *Convention on the Registration of Objects Launched into Outer Space* and General Assembly resolution 1721 (XVI) B of 20 December 1961. The Office also actively gathers and disseminates information on the status of the United Nations treaties on outer space, promotes the treaties, and circulates the Secretary-General's letters encouraging States and relevant international intergovernmental organizations to accede to them.

To summarize, since the outset of the involvement of the United Nations in space matters, the above-mentioned activities of the Office—along with many other activities—have aimed at pursuing proactive and creative measures to strengthen and effectively apply international space law for the benefit of all actors, including States and international intergovernmental and non-governmental organizations.

The present booklet is entitled *International Space Law: United Nations Instruments* as it represents the most comprehensive and up-to-date volume of instruments that have been developed, promoted and strengthened under the auspices of the United Nations. These instruments constitute the principal body of international space law and will continue to provide, further into the twenty-first century, an effective framework for the expanding and increasingly complex tasks aimed at the exploration and use of outer space for peaceful purposes. May they continue to support humankind's space activities throughout the years to come.

Simonetta Di Pippo
Director
United Nations
Office for Outer Space Affairs

Contents

Page

Part one. United Nations treaties **1**

A. Treaty on Principles Governing the Activities of States in the Exploration and Use of Outer Space, including the Moon and Other Celestial Bodies 3

B. Agreement on the Rescue of Astronauts, the Return of Astronauts and Return of Objects Launched into Outer Space 10

C. Convention on International Liability for Damage Caused by Space Objects 14

D. Convention on Registration of Objects Launched into Outer Space ... 24

E. Agreement Governing the Activities of States on the Moon and Other Celestial Bodies 30

F. United Nations treaties depositary information 40

Part two. Principles adopted by the General Assembly **43**

A. Declaration of Legal Principles Governing the Activities of States in the Exploration and Use of Outer Space 45

B. Principles Governing the Use by States of Artificial Earth Satellites for International Direct Television Broadcasting 48

C. Principles Relating to Remote Sensing of the Earth from Outer Space .. 52

D. Principles Relevant to the Use of Nuclear Power Sources in Outer Space 57

E. Declaration on International Cooperation in the Exploration and Use of Outer Space for the Benefit and in the Interest of All States, Taking into Particular Account the Needs of Developing Countries.... 65

Part three. Related resolutions adopted by the General Assembly **69**

A. Resolution 1721 A and B (XVI) of 20 December 1961: International cooperation in the peaceful uses of outer space 71

B. Paragraph 4 of resolution 55/122 of 8 December 2000: International cooperation in the peaceful uses of outer space 73

Some aspects concerning the use of the geostationary orbit 73

Page

C. Resolution 59/115 of 10 December 2004: Application of the concept of the "launching State" 76

D. Resolution 62/101 of 17 December 2007: Recommendations on enhancing the practice of States and international intergovernmental organizations in registering space objects 78

E. Resolution 68/74 of 11 December 2013: Recommendations on national legislation relevant to the peaceful exploration and use of outer space . . 83

Part four. Other documents **87**

A. Space Debris Mitigation Guidelines of the Committee on the Peaceful Uses of Outer Space 89

B. Safety Framework for Nuclear Power Source Applications in Outer Space. 94

Part one

United Nations treaties

A. Treaty on Principles Governing the Activities of States in the Exploration and Use of Outer Space, including the Moon and Other Celestial Bodies[1]

The States Parties to this Treaty,

Inspired by the great prospects opening up before mankind as a result of man's entry into outer space,

Recognizing the common interest of all mankind in the progress of the exploration and use of outer space for peaceful purposes,

Believing that the exploration and use of outer space should be carried on for the benefit of all peoples irrespective of the degree of their economic or scientific development,

Desiring to contribute to broad international cooperation in the scientific as well as the legal aspects of the exploration and use of outer space for peaceful purposes,

Believing that such cooperation will contribute to the development of mutual understanding and to the strengthening of friendly relations between States and peoples,

Recalling resolution 1962 (XVIII), entitled "Declaration of Legal Principles Governing the Activities of States in the Exploration and Use of Outer Space", which was adopted unanimously by the United Nations General Assembly on 13 December 1963,

Recalling resolution 1884 (XVIII), calling upon States to refrain from placing in orbit around the Earth any objects carrying nuclear weapons or any other kinds of weapons of mass destruction or from installing such weapons on celestial bodies, which was adopted unanimously by the United Nations General Assembly on 17 October 1963,

[1]United Nations, *Treaty Series,* vol. 610, No. 8843.

Taking account of United Nations General Assembly resolution 110 (II) of 3 November 1947, which condemned propaganda designed or likely to provoke or encourage any threat to the peace, breach of the peace or act of aggression, and considering that the aforementioned resolution is applicable to outer space,

Convinced that a Treaty on Principles Governing the Activities of States in the Exploration and Use of Outer Space, including the Moon and Other Celestial Bodies, will further the purposes and principles of the Charter of the United Nations,

Have agreed on the following:

Article I

The exploration and use of outer space, including the Moon and other celestial bodies, shall be carried out for the benefit and in the interests of all countries, irrespective of their degree of economic or scientific development, and shall be the province of all mankind.

Outer space, including the Moon and other celestial bodies, shall be free for exploration and use by all States without discrimination of any kind, on a basis of equality and in accordance with international law, and there shall be free access to all areas of celestial bodies.

There shall be freedom of scientific investigation in outer space, including the Moon and other celestial bodies, and States shall facilitate and encourage international cooperation in such investigation.

Article II

Outer space, including the Moon and other celestial bodies, is not subject to national appropriation by claim of sovereignty, by means of use or occupation, or by any other means.

Article III

States Parties to the Treaty shall carry on activities in the exploration and use of outer space, including the Moon and other celestial bodies, in accordance with international law, including the Charter of the United Nations, in the interest of maintaining international peace and security and promoting international cooperation and understanding.

Article IV

States Parties to the Treaty undertake not to place in orbit around the Earth any objects carrying nuclear weapons or any other kinds of weapons of mass destruction, install such weapons on celestial bodies, or station such weapons in outer space in any other manner.

The Moon and other celestial bodies shall be used by all States Parties to the Treaty exclusively for peaceful purposes. The establishment of military bases, installations and fortifications, the testing of any type of weapons and the conduct of military manoeuvres on celestial bodies shall be forbidden. The use of military personnel for scientific research or for any other peaceful purposes shall not be prohibited. The use of any equipment or facility necessary for peaceful exploration of the Moon and other celestial bodies shall also not be prohibited.

Article V

States Parties to the Treaty shall regard astronauts as envoys of mankind in outer space and shall render to them all possible assistance in the event of accident, distress, or emergency landing on the territory of another State Party or on the high seas. When astronauts make such a landing, they shall be safely and promptly returned to the State of registry of their space vehicle.

In carrying on activities in outer space and on celestial bodies, the astronauts of one State Party shall render all possible assistance to the astronauts of other States Parties.

States Parties to the Treaty shall immediately inform the other States Parties to the Treaty or the Secretary-General of the United Nations of any phenomena they discover in outer space, including the Moon and other celestial bodies, which could constitute a danger to the life or health of astronauts.

Article VI

States Parties to the Treaty shall bear international responsibility for national activities in outer space, including the Moon and other celestial bodies, whether such activities are carried on by governmental agencies or by non-governmental entities, and for assuring that national activities are carried out in conformity with the provisions set forth in the present Treaty. The activities of non-governmental entities in outer space, including the Moon and other celestial bodies, shall require authorization and continuing supervision by the appropriate State Party to the Treaty. When activities are carried on in outer space, including the Moon and other celestial bodies, by an international organization, responsibility for compliance with this Treaty shall be borne both by the international organization and by the States Parties to the Treaty participating in such organization.

Article VII

Each State Party to the Treaty that launches or procures the launching of an object into outer space, including the Moon and other celestial bodies, and each State Party from whose territory or facility an object is launched, is internationally liable for damage to another State Party to the Treaty or to its natural or juridical persons by such object or its component parts on the Earth, in air space or in outer space, including the Moon and other celestial bodies.

Article VIII

A State Party to the Treaty on whose registry an object launched into outer space is carried shall retain jurisdiction and control over such object, and over any personnel thereof, while in outer space or on a celestial body. Ownership of objects launched into outer space, including objects landed or constructed on a celestial body, and of their component parts, is not affected by their presence in outer space or on a celestial body or by their return to the Earth. Such objects or component parts found beyond the limits of the State Party to the Treaty on whose registry they are carried shall be returned to that State Party, which shall, upon request, furnish identifying data prior to their return.

Article IX

In the exploration and use of outer space, including the Moon and other celestial bodies, States Parties to the Treaty shall be guided by the principle of cooperation and mutual assistance and shall conduct all their activities in outer space, including the Moon and other celestial bodies, with due regard to the corresponding interests of all other States Parties to the Treaty. States Parties to the Treaty shall pursue studies of outer space, including the Moon and other celestial bodies, and conduct exploration of them so as to avoid their harmful contamination and also adverse changes in the environment of the Earth resulting from the introduction of extraterrestrial matter and, where necessary, shall adopt appropriate measures for this purpose. If a State Party to the Treaty has reason to believe that an activity or experiment planned by it or its nationals in outer space, including the Moon and other celestial bodies, would cause potentially harmful interference with activities of other States Parties in the peaceful exploration and use of outer space, including the Moon and other celestial bodies, it shall undertake appropriate international consultations before proceeding with any such activity or experiment. A State Party to the Treaty which has reason to believe that an activity or experiment planned by another State Party in outer space, including the Moon and other celestial bodies, would cause potentially harmful interference with activities in the peaceful exploration and use of outer space, including the Moon and other celestial bodies, may request consultation concerning the activity or experiment.

Article X

In order to promote international cooperation in the exploration and use of outer space, including the Moon and other celestial bodies, in conformity with the purposes of this Treaty, the States Parties to the Treaty shall consider on a basis of equality any requests by other States Parties to the Treaty to be afforded an opportunity to observe the flight of space objects launched by those States.

The nature of such an opportunity for observation and the conditions under which it could be afforded shall be determined by agreement between the States concerned.

Article XI

In order to promote international cooperation in the peaceful exploration and use of outer space, States Parties to the Treaty conducting activities in outer space, including the Moon and other celestial bodies, agree to inform the Secretary-General of the United Nations as well as the public and the international scientific community, to the greatest extent feasible and practicable, of the nature, conduct, locations and results of such activities. On receiving the said information, the Secretary-General of the United Nations should be prepared to disseminate it immediately and effectively.

Article XII

All stations, installations, equipment and space vehicles on the Moon and other celestial bodies shall be open to representatives of other States Parties to the Treaty on a basis of reciprocity. Such representatives shall give reasonable advance notice of a projected visit, in order that appropriate consultations may be held and that maximum precautions may be taken to assure safety and to avoid interference with normal operations in the facility to be visited.

Article XIII

The provisions of this Treaty shall apply to the activities of States Parties to the Treaty in the exploration and use of outer space, including the Moon and other celestial bodies, whether such activities are carried on by a single State Party to the Treaty or jointly with other States, including cases where they are carried on within the framework of international intergovernmental organizations.

Any practical questions arising in connection with activities carried on by international intergovernmental organizations in the exploration and use of outer space, including the Moon and other celestial bodies, shall be resolved by the States Parties to the Treaty either with the appropriate international organization or with one or more States members of that international organization, which are Parties to this Treaty.

Article XIV

1. This Treaty shall be open to all States for signature. Any State which does not sign this Treaty before its entry into force in accordance with paragraph 3 of this article may accede to it at any time.

2. This Treaty shall be subject to ratification by signatory States. Instruments of ratification and instruments of accession shall be deposited with the Governments of the Union of Soviet Socialist Republics, the United Kingdom of Great Britain and Northern Ireland and the United States of America, which are hereby designated the Depositary Governments.

3. This Treaty shall enter into force upon the deposit of instruments of ratification by five Governments including the Governments designated as Depositary Governments under this Treaty.

4. For States whose instruments of ratification or accession are deposited subsequent to the entry into force of this Treaty, it shall enter into force on the date of the deposit of their instruments of ratification or accession.

5. The Depositary Governments shall promptly inform all signatory and acceding States of the date of each signature, the date of deposit of each instrument of ratification of and accession to this Treaty, the date of its entry into force and other notices.

6. This Treaty shall be registered by the Depositary Governments pursuant to Article 102 of the Charter of the United Nations.

Article XV

Any State Party to the Treaty may propose amendments to this Treaty. Amendments shall enter into force for each State Party to the Treaty accepting the amendments upon their acceptance by a majority of the States Parties to the Treaty and thereafter for each remaining State Party to the Treaty on the date of acceptance by it.

Article XVI

Any State Party to the Treaty may give notice of its withdrawal from the Treaty one year after its entry into force by written notification to the Depositary Governments. Such withdrawal shall take effect one year from the date of receipt of this notification.

Article XVII

This Treaty, of which the Chinese, English, French, Russian and Spanish texts are equally authentic, shall be deposited in the archives of the Depositary Governments. Duly certified copies of this Treaty shall be transmitted by the Depositary Governments to the Governments of the signatory and acceding States.

IN WITNESS WHEREOF the undersigned, duly authorized, have signed this Treaty.

DONE in triplicate, at the cities of London, Moscow and Washington, D.C., the twenty-seventh day of January, one thousand nine hundred and sixty-seven.

B. Agreement on the Rescue of Astronauts, the Return of Astronauts and Return of Objects Launched into Outer Space[2]

The Contracting Parties,

Noting the great importance of the Treaty on Principles Governing the Activities of States in the Exploration and Use of Outer Space, including the Moon and Other Celestial Bodies,[1] which calls for the rendering of all possible assistance to astronauts in the event of accident, distress or emergency landing, the prompt and safe return of astronauts, and the return of objects launched into outer space,

Desiring to develop and give further concrete expression to these duties,

Wishing to promote international cooperation in the peaceful exploration and use of outer space,

Prompted by sentiments of humanity,

Have agreed on the following:

Article 1

Each Contracting Party which receives information or discovers that the personnel of a spacecraft have suffered accident or are experiencing conditions of distress or have made an emergency or unintended landing in territory under its jurisdiction or on the high seas or in any other place not under the jurisdiction of any State shall immediately:

(a) Notify the launching authority or, if it cannot identify and immediately communicate with the launching authority, immediately make a public announcement by all appropriate means of communication at its disposal;

(b) Notify the Secretary-General of the United Nations, who should disseminate the information without delay by all appropriate means of communication at his disposal.

---

[2]United Nations, *Treaty Series,* vol. 672, No. 9574.

Article 2

If, owing to accident, distress, emergency or unintended landing, the personnel of a spacecraft land in territory under the jurisdiction of a Contracting Party, it shall immediately take all possible steps to rescue them and render them all necessary assistance. It shall inform the launching authority and also the Secretary-General of the United Nations of the steps it is taking and of their progress. If assistance by the launching authority would help to effect a prompt rescue or would contribute substantially to the effectiveness of search and rescue operations, the launching authority shall cooperate with the Contracting Party with a view to the effective conduct of search and rescue operations. Such operations shall be subject to the direction and control of the Contracting Party, which shall act in close and continuing consultation with the launching authority.

Article 3

If information is received or it is discovered that the personnel of a spacecraft have alighted on the high seas or in any other place not under the jurisdiction of any State, those Contracting Parties which are in a position to do so shall, if necessary, extend assistance in search and rescue operations for such personnel to assure their speedy rescue. They shall inform the launching authority and the Secretary-General of the United Nations of the steps they are taking and of their progress.

Article 4

If, owing to accident, distress, emergency or unintended landing, the personnel of a spacecraft land in territory under the jurisdiction of a Contracting Party or have been found on the high seas or in any other place not under the jurisdiction of any State, they shall be safely and promptly returned to representatives of the launching authority.

Article 5

1. Each Contracting Party which receives information or discovers that a space object or its component parts has returned to Earth in territory under its jurisdiction or on the high seas or in any other place not under the jurisdiction of any State, shall notify the launching authority and the Secretary-General of the United Nations.

2. Each Contracting Party having jurisdiction over the territory on which a space object or its component parts has been discovered shall, upon the request of the launching authority and with assistance from that authority if requested, take such steps as it finds practicable to recover the object or component parts.

3. Upon request of the launching authority, objects launched into outer space or their component parts found beyond the territorial limits of the launching authority shall be returned to or held at the disposal of representatives of the launching authority, which shall, upon request, furnish identifying data prior to their return.

4. Notwithstanding paragraphs 2 and 3 of this article, a Contracting Party which has reason to believe that a space object or its component parts discovered in territory under its jurisdiction, or recovered by it elsewhere, is of a hazardous or deleterious nature may so notify the launching authority, which shall immediately take effective steps, under the direction and control of the said Contracting Party, to eliminate possible danger of harm.

5. Expenses incurred in fulfilling obligations to recover and return a space object or its component parts under paragraphs 2 and 3 of this article shall be borne by the launching authority.

Article 6

For the purposes of this Agreement, the term "launching authority" shall refer to the State responsible for launching, or, where an international intergovernmental organization is responsible for launching, that organization, provided that that organization declares its acceptance of the rights and obligations provided for in this Agreement and a majority of the States members of that organization are Contracting Parties to this Agreement and to the Treaty on Principles Governing the Activities of States in the Exploration and Use of Outer Space, including the Moon and Other Celestial Bodies.

Article 7

1. This Agreement shall be open to all States for signature. Any State which does not sign this Agreement before its entry into force in accordance with paragraph 3 of this article may accede to it at any time.

2. This Agreement shall be subject to ratification by signatory States. Instruments of ratification and instruments of accession shall be deposited with the Governments of the Union of Soviet Socialist Republics, the United Kingdom of Great Britain and Northern Ireland and the United States of America, which are hereby designated the Depositary Governments.

3. This Agreement shall enter into force upon the deposit of instruments of ratification by five Governments including the Governments designated as Depositary Governments under this Agreement.

4. For States whose instruments of ratification or accession are deposited subsequent to the entry into force of this Agreement, it shall enter into force on the date of the deposit of their instruments of ratification or accession.

5. The Depositary Governments shall promptly inform all signatory and acceding States of the date of each signature, the date of deposit of each instrument of ratification of and accession to this Agreement, the date of its entry into force and other notices.

6. This Agreement shall be registered by the Depositary Governments pursuant to Article 102 of the Charter of the United Nations.

Article 8

Any State Party to the Agreement may propose amendments to this Agreement. Amendments shall enter into force for each State Party to the Agreement accepting the amendments upon their acceptance by a majority of the States Parties to the Agreement and thereafter for each remaining State Party to the Agreement on the date of acceptance by it.

Article 9

Any State Party to the Agreement may give notice of its withdrawal from the Agreement one year after its entry into force by written notification to the Depositary Governments. Such withdrawal shall take effect one year from the date of receipt of this notification.

Article 10

This Agreement, of which the Chinese, English, French, Russian and Spanish texts are equally authentic, shall be deposited in the archives of the Depositary Governments. Duly certified copies of this Agreement shall be transmitted by the Depositary Governments to the Governments of the signatory and acceding States.

IN WITNESS WHEREOF the undersigned, duly authorized, have signed this Agreement.

DONE in triplicate, at the cities of London, Moscow and Washington, D.C., the twenty-second day of April, one thousand nine hundred and sixty-eight.

C. Convention on International Liability for Damage Caused by Space Objects[3]

The State Parties to this Convention,

Recognizing the common interest of all mankind in furthering the exploration and use of outer space for peaceful purposes,

Recalling the Treaty on Principles Governing the Activities of States in the Exploration and Use of Outer Space, including the Moon and Other Celestial Bodies,

Taking into consideration that, notwithstanding the precautionary measures to be taken by States and international intergovernmental organizations involved in the launching of space objects, damage may on occasion be caused by such objects,

Recognizing the need to elaborate effective international rules and procedures concerning liability for damage caused by space objects and to ensure, in particular, the prompt payment under the terms of this Convention of a full and equitable measure of compensation to victims of such damage,

Believing that the establishment of such rules and procedures will contribute to the strengthening of international cooperation in the field of the exploration and use of outer space for peaceful purposes,

Have agreed on the following:

Article I

For the purposes of this Convention:

(a) The term "damage" means loss of life, personal injury or other impairment of health; or loss of or damage to property of States or of persons, natural or juridical, or property of international intergovernmental organizations;

(b) The term "launching" includes attempted launching;

[3]United Nations, *Treaty Series,* vol. 961, No. 13810.

(c) The term "launching State" means:

(i) A State which launches or procures the launching of a space object;

(ii) A state from whose territory or facility a space object is launched;

(d) The term "space object" includes component parts of a space object as well as its launch vehicle and parts thereof.

Article II

A launching State shall be absolutely liable to pay compensation for damage caused by its space object on the surface of the Earth or to aircraft in flight.

Article III

In the event of damage being caused elsewhere than on the surface of the Earth to a space object of one launching State or to persons or property on board such a space object by a space object of another launching State, the latter shall be liable only if the damage is due to its fault or the fault of persons for whom it is responsible.

Article IV

1. In the event of damage being caused elsewhere than on the surface of the Earth to a space object of one launching State or to persons or property on board such a space object by a space object of another launching State, and of damage thereby being caused to a third State or to its natural or juridical persons, the first two States shall be jointly and severally liable to the third State, to the extent indicated by the following:

(a) If the damage has been caused to the third State on the surface of the Earth or to aircraft in flight, their liability to the third State shall be absolute;

(b) If the damage has been caused to a space object of the third State or to persons or property on board that space object elsewhere than on the surface of the Earth, their liability to the third State shall be based on the fault of either of the first two States or on the fault of persons for whom either is responsible.

2. In all cases of joint and several liability referred to in paragraph 1 of this article, the burden of compensation for the damage shall be apportioned between the first two States in accordance with the extent to which they were at fault; if the extent of the fault of each of these States cannot be established, the burden of compensation shall be apportioned equally between them. Such apportionment shall be without prejudice to the right of the third State to seek the entire compensation due under this Convention from any or all of the launching States which are jointly and severally liable.

Article V

1. Whenever two or more States jointly launch a space object, they shall be jointly and severally liable for any damage caused.

2. A launching State which has paid compensation for damage shall have the right to present a claim for indemnification to other participants in the joint launching. The participants in a joint launching may conclude agreements regarding the apportioning among themselves of the financial obligation in respect of which they are jointly and severally liable. Such agreements shall be without prejudice to the right of a State sustaining damage to seek the entire compensation due under this Convention from any or all of the launching States which are jointly and severally liable.

3. A State from whose territory or facility a space object is launched shall be regarded as a participant in a joint launching.

Article VI

1. Subject to the provisions of paragraph 2 of this article, exoneration from absolute liability shall be granted to the extent that a launching State establishes that the damage has resulted either wholly or partially from gross negligence or from an act or omission done with intent to cause damage on the part of a claimant State or of natural or juridical persons it represents.

2. No exoneration whatever shall be granted in cases where the damage has resulted from activities conducted by a launching State which are not in conformity with international law including, in particular, the Charter of the United Nations and the Treaty on Principles Governing the Activities of States in the Exploration and Use of Outer Space, including the Moon and Other Celestial Bodies.

Article VII

The provisions of this Convention shall not apply to damage caused by a space object of a launching State to:

(a) Nationals of that launching State;

(b) Foreign nationals during such time as they are participating in the operation of that space object from the time of its launching or at any stage thereafter until its descent, or during such time as they are in the immediate vicinity of a planned launching or recovery area as the result of an invitation by that launching State.

Article VIII

1. A State which suffers damage, or whose natural or juridical persons suffer damage, may present to a launching State a claim for compensation for such damage.

2. If the State of nationality has not presented a claim, another State may, in respect of damage sustained in its territory by any natural or juridical person, present a claim to a launching State.

3. If neither the State of nationality nor the State in whose territory the damage was sustained has presented a claim or notified its intention of presenting a claim, another State may, in respect of damage sustained by its permanent residents, present a claim to a launching State.

Article IX

A claim for compensation for damage shall be presented to a launching State through diplomatic channels. If a State does not maintain diplomatic relations with the launching State concerned, it may request another State to present its claim to that launching State or otherwise represent its interests under this Convention. It may also present its claim through the Secretary-General of the United Nations, provided the claimant State and the launching State are both Members of the United Nations.

Article X

1. A claim for compensation for damage may be presented to a launching State not later than one year following the date of the occurrence of the damage or the identification of the launching State which is liable.

2. If, however, a State does not know of the occurrence of the damage or has not been able to identify the launching State which is liable, it may present a claim within one year following the date on which it learned of the aforementioned facts; however, this period shall in no event exceed one year following the date on which the State could reasonably be expected to have learned of the facts through the exercise of due diligence.

3. The time limits specified in paragraphs 1 and 2 of this article shall apply even if the full extent of the damage may not be known. In this event, however, the claimant State shall be entitled to revise the claim and submit additional documentation after the expiration of such time limits until one year after the full extent of the damage is known.

Article XI

1. Presentation of a claim to a launching State for compensation for damage under this Convention shall not require the prior exhaustion of any local remedies which may be available to a claimant State or to natural or juridical persons it represents.

2. Nothing in this Convention shall prevent a State, or natural or juridical persons it might represent, from pursuing a claim in the courts or administrative tribunals or agencies of a launching State. A State shall not, however, be entitled to present a claim under this Convention in respect of the same damage for which a claim is being pursued in the courts or administrative tribunals or agencies of a launching State or under another international agreement which is binding on the States concerned.

Article XII

The compensation which the launching State shall be liable to pay for damage under this Convention shall be determined in accordance with international law and the principles of justice and equity, in order to provide such reparation in respect of the damage as will restore the person, natural or juridical, State or international organization on whose behalf the claim is presented to the condition which would have existed if the damage had not occurred.

Article XIII

Unless the claimant State and the State from which compensation is due under this Convention agree on another form of compensation, the compensation shall be paid in the currency of the claimant State or, if that State so requests, in the currency of the State from which compensation is due.

Article XIV

If no settlement of a claim is arrived at through diplomatic negotiations as provided for in article IX, within one year from the date on which the claimant State notifies the launching State that it has submitted the documentation of its claim, the parties concerned shall establish a Claims Commission at the request of either party.

Article XV

1. The Claims Commission shall be composed of three members: one appointed by the claimant State, one appointed by the launching State and the third member, the Chairman, to be chosen by both parties jointly. Each party shall make its appointment within two months of the request for the establishment of the Claims Commission.

2. If no agreement is reached on the choice of the Chairman within four months of the request for the establishment of the Commission, either party may request the Secretary-General of the United Nations to appoint the Chairman within a further period of two months.

Article XVI

1. If one of the parties does not make its appointment within the stipulated period, the Chairman shall, at the request of the other party, constitute a single-member Claims Commission.

2. Any vacancy which may arise in the Commission for whatever reason shall be filled by the same procedure adopted for the original appointment.

3. The Commission shall determine its own procedure.

4. The Commission shall determine the place or places where it shall sit and all other administrative matters.

5. Except in the case of decisions and awards by a single-member Commission, all decisions and awards of the Commission shall be by majority vote.

Article XVII

No increase in the membership of the Claims Commission shall take place by reason of two or more claimant States or launching States being joined in any one proceeding before the Commission. The claimant States so joined shall collectively appoint one member of the Commission in the same manner and subject to the same conditions as would be the case for a single claimant State. When two or more launching States are so joined, they shall collectively appoint one member of the Commission in the same way. If the claimant States or the launching States do not make the appointment within the stipulated period, the Chairman shall constitute a single-member Commission.

Article XVIII

The Claims Commission shall decide the merits of the claim for compensation and determine the amount of compensation payable, if any.

Article XIX

1. The Claims Commission shall act in accordance with the provisions of article XII.

2. The decision of the Commission shall be final and binding if the parties have so agreed; otherwise the Commission shall render a final and recommendatory award, which the parties shall consider in good faith. The Commission shall state the reasons for its decision or award.

3. The Commission shall give its decision or award as promptly as possible and no later than one year from the date of its establishment, unless an extension of this period is found necessary by the Commission.

4. The Commission shall make its decision or award public. It shall deliver a certified copy of its decision or award to each of the parties and to the Secretary-General of the United Nations.

Article XX

The expenses in regard to the Claims Commission shall be borne equally by the parties, unless otherwise decided by the Commission.

Article XXI

If the damage caused by a space object presents a large-scale danger to human life or seriously interferes with the living conditions of the population or the functioning of vital centres, the States Parties, and in particular the launching State, shall examine the possibility of rendering appropriate and rapid assistance to the State which has suffered the damage, when it so requests.

However, nothing in this article shall affect the rights or obligations of the States Parties under this Convention.

Article XXII

1. In this Convention, with the exception of articles XXIV to XXVII, references to States shall be deemed to apply to any international intergovernmental organization which conducts space activities if the organization declares its acceptance of the rights and obligations provided for in this Convention and if a majority of the States members of the organization are States Parties to this Convention and to the Treaty on Principles Governing the Activities of States in the Exploration and Use of Outer Space, including the Moon and Other Celestial Bodies.

2. States members of any such organization which are States Parties to this Convention shall take all appropriate steps to ensure that the organization makes a declaration in accordance with the preceding paragraph.

3. If an international intergovernmental organization is liable for damage by virtue of the provisions of this Convention, that organization and those of its members which are States Parties to this Convention shall be jointly and severally liable; provided, however, that:

(a) Any claim for compensation in respect of such damage shall be first presented to the organization;

(b) Only where the organization has not paid, within a period of six months, any sum agreed or determined to be due as compensation for such damage, may the claimant State invoke the liability of the members which are States Parties to this Convention for the payment of that sum.

4. Any claim, pursuant to the provisions of this Convention, for compensation in respect of damage caused to an organization which has made a declaration in accordance with paragraph 1 of this article shall be presented by a State member of the organization which is a State Party to this Convention.

Article XXIII

1. The provisions of this Convention shall not affect other international agreements in force insofar as relations between the States Parties to such agreements are concerned.

2. No provision of this Convention shall prevent States from concluding international agreements reaffirming, supplementing or extending its provisions.

Article XXIV

1. This Convention shall be open to all States for signature. Any State which does not sign this Convention before its entry into force in accordance with paragraph 3 of this article may accede to it at any time.

2. This Convention shall be subject to ratification by signatory States. Instruments of ratification and instruments of accession shall be deposited with the Governments of the Union of Soviet Socialist Republics, the United Kingdom of Great Britain and Northern Ireland and the United States of America, which are hereby designated the Depositary Governments.

3. This Convention shall enter into force on the deposit of the fifth instrument of ratification.

4. For States whose instruments of ratification or accession are deposited subsequent to the entry into force of this Convention, it shall enter into force on the date of the deposit of their instruments of ratification or accession.

5. The Depositary Governments shall promptly inform all signatory and acceding States of the date of each signature, the date of deposit of each instrument of ratification of and accession to this Convention, the date of its entry into force and other notices.

6. This Convention shall be registered by the Depositary Governments pursuant to Article 102 of the Charter of the United Nations.

Article XXV

Any State Party to this Convention may propose amendments to this Convention. Amendments shall enter into force for each State Party to the Convention accepting the amendments upon their acceptance by a majority of the States Parties to the Convention and thereafter for each remaining State Party to the Convention on the date of acceptance by it.

Article XXVI

Ten years after the entry into force of this Convention, the question of the review of this Convention shall be included in the provisional agenda of the United Nations General Assembly in order to consider, in the light of past application of the Convention, whether it requires revision. However, at any time after the Convention has been in force for five years, and at the request of one third of the States Parties to the Convention, and with the concurrence of the majority of the States Parties, a conference of the States Parties shall be convened to review this Convention.

Article XXVII

Any State Party to this Convention may give notice of its withdrawal from the Convention one year after its entry into force by written notification to the Depositary Governments. Such withdrawal shall take effect one year from the date of receipt of this notification.

Article XXVIII

This Convention, of which the Chinese, English, French, Russian and Spanish texts are equally authentic, shall be deposited in the archives of the Depositary Governments. Duly certified copies of this Convention shall be transmitted by the Depositary Governments to the Governments of the signatory and acceding States.

IN WITNESS WHEREOF the undersigned, duly authorized thereto, have signed this Convention.

DONE in triplicate, at the cities of London, Moscow and Washington, D.C., this twenty-ninth day of March, one thousand nine hundred and seventy-two.

D. Convention on Registration of Objects Launched into Outer Space[4]

The State Parties to this Convention,

Recognizing the common interest of all mankind in furthering the exploration and use of outer space for peaceful purposes,

Recalling that the Treaty on Principles Governing the Activities of States in the Exploration and Use of Outer Space, including the Moon and Other Celestial Bodies,[1] of 27 January 1967 affirms that States shall bear international responsibility for their national activities in outer space and refers to the State on whose registry an object launched into outer space is carried,

Recalling also that the Agreement on the Rescue of Astronauts, the Return of Astronauts and the Return of Objects Launched into Outer Space[2] of 22 April 1968 provides that a launching authority shall, upon request, furnish identifying data prior to the return of an object it has launched into outer space found beyond the territorial limits of the launching authority,

Recalling further that the Convention on International Liability for Damage Caused by Space Objects[3] of 29 March 1972 establishes international rules and procedures concerning the liability of launching States for damage caused by their space objects,

Desiring, in the light of the Treaty on Principles Governing the Activities of States in the Exploration and Use of Outer Space, including the Moon and Other Celestial Bodies, to make provision for the national registration by launching States of space objects launched into outer space,

Desiring further that a central register of objects launched into outer space be established and maintained, on a mandatory basis, by the Secretary-General of the United Nations,

Desiring also to provide for States Parties additional means and procedures to assist in the identification of space objects,

Believing that a mandatory system of registering objects launched into outer space would, in particular, assist in their identification and would contribute

[4]United Nations, *Treaty Series,* vol. 1023, No. 15020.

to the application and development of international law governing the exploration and use of outer space,

Have agreed on the following:

Article I

For the purposes of this Convention:

(a) The term "launching State" means:

(i) A State which launches or procures the launching of a space object;

(ii) A State from whose territory or facility a space object is launched;

(b) The term "space object" includes component parts of a space object as well as its launch vehicle and parts thereof;

(c) The term "State of registry" means a launching State on whose registry a space object is carried in accordance with article II.

Article II

1. When a space object is launched into Earth orbit or beyond, the launching State shall register the space object by means of an entry in an appropriate registry which it shall maintain. Each launching State shall inform the Secretary-General of the United Nations of the establishment of such a registry.

2. Where there are two or more launching States in respect of any such space object, they shall jointly determine which one of them shall register the object in accordance with paragraph 1 of this article, bearing in mind the provisions of article VIII of the Treaty on Principles Governing the Activities of States in the Exploration and Use of Outer Space, including the Moon and Other Celestial Bodies, and without prejudice to appropriate agreements concluded or to be concluded among the launching States on jurisdiction and control over the space object and over any personnel thereof.

3. The contents of each registry and the conditions under which it is maintained shall be determined by the State of registry concerned.

Article III

1. The Secretary-General of the United Nations shall maintain a Register in which the information furnished in accordance with article IV shall be recorded.

2. There shall be full and open access to the information in this Register.

Article IV

1. Each State of registry shall furnish to the Secretary-General of the United Nations, as soon as practicable, the following information concerning each space object carried on its registry:

(a) Name of launching State or States;

(b) An appropriate designator of the space object or its registration number;

(c) Date and territory or location of launch;

(d) Basic orbital parameters, including:

(i) Nodal period;
(ii) Inclination;
(iii) Apogee;
(iv) Perigee;

(e) General function of the space object.

2. Each State of registry may, from time to time, provide the Secretary-General of the United Nations with additional information concerning a space object carried on its registry.

3. Each State of registry shall notify the Secretary-General of the United Nations, to the greatest extent feasible and as soon as practicable, of space objects concerning which it has previously transmitted information, and which have been but no longer are in Earth orbit.

Article V

Whenever a space object launched into Earth orbit or beyond is marked with the designator or registration number referred to in article IV, paragraph 1 *(b)*, or both, the State of registry shall notify the Secretary-General of this fact when submitting the information regarding the space object in accordance with article IV. In such case, the Secretary-General of the United Nations shall record this notification in the Register.

Article VI

Where the application of the provisions of this Convention has not enabled a State Party to identify a space object which has caused damage to it or to any of its natural or juridical persons, or which may be of a hazardous or deleterious nature, other States Parties, including in particular States possessing space monitoring and tracking facilities, shall respond to the greatest extent feasible to a request by that State Party, or transmitted through the Secretary-General on its behalf, for assistance under equitable and reasonable conditions in the identification of the object. A State Party making such a request shall, to the greatest extent feasible, submit information as to the time, nature and circumstances of the events giving rise to the request. Arrangements under which such assistance shall be rendered shall be the subject of agreement between the parties concerned.

Article VII

1. In this Convention, with the exception of articles VIII to XII inclusive, references to States shall be deemed to apply to any international intergovernmental organization which conducts space activities if the organization declares its acceptance of the rights and obligations provided for in this Convention and if a majority of the States members of the organization are States Parties to this Convention and to the Treaty on Principles Governing the Activities of States in the Exploration and Use of Outer Space, including the Moon and Other Celestial Bodies.

2. States members of any such organization which are States Parties to this Convention shall take all appropriate steps to ensure that the organization makes a declaration in accordance with paragraph 1 of this article.

Article VIII

1. This Convention shall be open for signature by all States at United Nations Headquarters in New York. Any State which does not sign this Convention before its entry into force in accordance with paragraph 3 of this article may accede to it at any time.

2. This Convention shall be subject to ratification by signatory States. Instruments of ratification and instruments of accession shall be deposited with the Secretary-General of the United Nations.

3. This Convention shall enter into force among the States which have deposited instruments of ratification on the deposit of the fifth such instrument with the Secretary-General of the United Nations.

4. For States whose instruments of ratification or accession are deposited subsequent to the entry into force of this Convention, it shall enter into force on the date of the deposit of their instruments of ratification or accession.

5. The Secretary-General shall promptly inform all signatory and acceding States of the date of each signature, the date of deposit of each instrument of ratification of and accession to this Convention, the date of its entry into force and other notices.

Article IX

Any State Party to this Convention may propose amendments to the Convention. Amendments shall enter into force for each State Party to the Convention accepting the amendments upon their acceptance by a majority of the States Parties to the Convention and thereafter for each remaining State Party to the Convention on the date of acceptance by it.

Article X

Ten years after the entry into force of this Convention, the question of the review of the Convention shall be included in the provisional agenda of the United Nations General Assembly in order to consider, in the light of past application of the Convention, whether it requires revision. However, at any time after the Convention has been in force for five years, at the request of one third of the States Parties to the Convention and with the concurrence of the majority of the States Parties, a conference of the States Parties shall be convened to review this Convention. Such review shall take into account in particular any relevant technological developments, including those relating to the identification of space objects.

Article XI

Any State Party to this Convention may give notice of its withdrawal from the Convention one year after its entry into force by written notification to the Secretary-General of the United Nations. Such withdrawal shall take effect one year from the date of receipt of this notification.

Article XII

The original of this Convention, of which the Arabic, Chinese, English, French, Russian and Spanish texts are equally authentic, shall be deposited with the Secretary-General of the United Nations, who shall send certified copies thereof to all signatory and acceding States.

IN WITNESS WHEREOF the undersigned, being duly authorized thereto by their respective Governments, have signed this Convention, opened for signature at New York on the fourteenth day of January, one thousand nine hundred and seventy-five.

E. Agreement Governing the Activities of States on the Moon and Other Celestial Bodies[5]

The States Parties to this Agreement,

Noting the achievements of States in the exploration and use of the Moon and other celestial bodies,

Recognizing that the Moon, as a natural satellite of the Earth, has an important role to play in the exploration of outer space,

Determined to promote on the basis of equality the further development of cooperation among States in the exploration and use of the Moon and other celestial bodies,

Desiring to prevent the Moon from becoming an area of international conflict,

Bearing in mind the benefits which may be derived from the exploitation of the natural resources of the Moon and other celestial bodies,

Recalling the Treaty on Principles Governing the Activities of States in the Exploration and Use of Outer Space, including the Moon and Other Celestial Bodies,[1] the Agreement on the Rescue of Astronauts, the Return of Astronauts and the Return of Objects Launched into Outer Space,[2] the Convention on International Liability for Damage Caused by Space Objects,[3] and the Convention on Registration of Objects Launched into Outer Space,[4]

Taking into account the need to define and develop the provisions of these international instruments in relation to the Moon and other celestial bodies, having regard to further progress in the exploration and use of outer space,

Have agreed on the following:

Article 1

1. The provisions of this Agreement relating to the Moon shall also apply to other celestial bodies within the solar system, other than the Earth, except

[5]United Nations, *Treaty Series,* vol. 1363, No. 23002.

insofar as specific legal norms enter into force with respect to any of these celestial bodies.

2. For the purposes of this Agreement reference to the Moon shall include orbits around or other trajectories to or around it.

3. This Agreement does not apply to extraterrestrial materials which reach the surface of the Earth by natural means.

Article 2

All activities on the Moon, including its exploration and use, shall be carried out in accordance with international law, in particular the Charter of the United Nations, and taking into account the Declaration on Principles of International Law concerning Friendly Relations and Cooperation among States in accordance with the Charter of the United Nations,[6] adopted by the General Assembly on 24 October 1970, in the interest of maintaining international peace and security and promoting international cooperation and mutual understanding, and with due regard to the corresponding interests of all other States Parties.

Article 3

1. The Moon shall be used by all States Parties exclusively for peaceful purposes.

2. Any threat or use of force or any other hostile act or threat of hostile act on the Moon is prohibited. It is likewise prohibited to use the Moon in order to commit any such act or to engage in any such threat in relation to the Earth, the Moon, spacecraft, the personnel of spacecraft or manmade space objects.

3. States Parties shall not place in orbit around or other trajectory to or around the Moon objects carrying nuclear weapons or any other kinds of weapons of mass destruction or place or use such weapons on or in the Moon.

4. The establishment of military bases, installations and fortifications, the testing of any type of weapons and the conduct of military manoeuvres on the Moon shall be forbidden. The use of military personnel for scientific research or for any other peaceful purposes shall not be prohibited. The use of any equipment or facility necessary for peaceful exploration and use of the Moon shall also not be prohibited.

---

[6]Resolution 2625 (XXV), annex.

Article 4

1. The exploration and use of the Moon shall be the province of all mankind and shall be carried out for the benefit and in the interests of all countries, irrespective of their degree of economic or scientific development. Due regard shall be paid to the interests of present and future generations as well as to the need to promote higher standards of living and conditions of economic and social progress and development in accordance with the Charter of the United Nations.

2. States Parties shall be guided by the principle of cooperation and mutual assistance in all their activities concerning the exploration and use of the Moon. International cooperation in pursuance of this Agreement should be as wide as possible and may take place on a multilateral basis, on a bilateral basis or through international intergovernmental organizations.

Article 5

1. States Parties shall inform the Secretary-General of the United Nations as well as the public and the international scientific community, to the greatest extent feasible and practicable, of their activities concerned with the exploration and use of the Moon. Information on the time, purposes, locations, orbital parameters and duration shall be given in respect of each mission to the Moon as soon as possible after launching, while information on the results of each mission, including scientific results, shall be furnished upon completion of the mission. In the case of a mission lasting more than sixty days, information on conduct of the mission, including any scientific results, shall be given periodically, at thirty-day intervals. For missions lasting more than six months, only significant additions to such information need be reported thereafter.

2. If a State Party becomes aware that another State Party plans to operate simultaneously in the same area of or in the same orbit around or trajectory to or around the Moon, it shall promptly inform the other State of the timing of and plans for its own operations.

3. In carrying out activities under this Agreement, States Parties shall promptly inform the Secretary-General, as well as the public and the international scientific community, of any phenomena they discover in outer space, including the Moon, which could endanger human life or health, as well as of any indication of organic life.

Article 6

1. There shall be freedom of scientific investigation on the Moon by all States Parties without discrimination of any kind, on the basis of equality and in accordance with international law.

2. In carrying out scientific investigations and in furtherance of the provisions of this Agreement, the States Parties shall have the right to collect on and remove from the Moon samples of its mineral and other substances. Such samples shall remain at the disposal of those States Parties which caused them to be collected and may be used by them for scientific purposes. States Parties shall have regard to the desirability of making a portion of such samples available to other interested States Parties and the international scientific community for scientific investigation. States Parties may in the course of scientific investigations also use mineral and other substances of the Moon in quantities appropriate for the support of their missions.

3. States Parties agree on the desirability of exchanging scientific and other personnel on expeditions to or installations on the Moon to the greatest extent feasible and practicable.

Article 7

1. In exploring and using the Moon, States Parties shall take measures to prevent the disruption of the existing balance of its environment, whether by introducing adverse changes in that environment, by its harmful contamination through the introduction of extra-environmental matter or otherwise. States Parties shall also take measures to avoid harmfully affecting the environment of the Earth through the introduction of extraterrestrial matter or otherwise.

2. States Parties shall inform the Secretary-General of the United Nations of the measures being adopted by them in accordance with paragraph 1 of this article and shall also, to the maximum extent feasible, notify him in advance of all placements by them of radioactive materials on the Moon and of the purposes of such placements.

3. States Parties shall report to other States Parties and to the Secretary-General concerning areas of the Moon having special scientific interest in order that, without prejudice to the rights of other States Parties, consideration may be given to the designation of such areas as international scientific preserves for which special protective arrangements are to be agreed upon in consultation with the competent bodies of the United Nations.

Article 8

1. States Parties may pursue their activities in the exploration and use of the Moon anywhere on or below its surface, subject to the provisions of this Agreement.

2. For these purposes States Parties may, in particular:

(a) Land their space objects on the Moon and launch them from the Moon;

(b) Place their personnel, space vehicles, equipment, facilities, stations and installations anywhere on or below the surface of the Moon.

Personnel, space vehicles, equipment, facilities, stations and installations may move or be moved freely over or below the surface of the Moon.

3. Activities of States Parties in accordance with paragraphs 1 and 2 of this article shall not interfere with the activities of other States Parties on the Moon. Where such interference may occur, the States Parties concerned shall undertake consultations in accordance with article 15, paragraphs 2 and 3, of this Agreement.

Article 9

1. States Parties may establish manned and unmanned stations on the Moon. A State Party establishing a station shall use only that area which is required for the needs of the station and shall immediately inform the Secretary-General of the United Nations of the location and purposes of that station. Subsequently, at annual intervals that State shall likewise inform the Secretary-General whether the station continues in use and whether its purposes have changed.

2. Stations shall be installed in such a manner that they do not impede the free access to all areas of the Moon of personnel, vehicles and equipment of other States Parties conducting activities on the Moon in accordance with the provisions of this Agreement or of article I of the Treaty on Principles Governing the Activities of States in the Exploration and Use of Outer Space, including the Moon and Other Celestial Bodies.

Article 10

1. States Parties shall adopt all practicable measures to safeguard the life and health of persons on the Moon. For this purpose they shall regard any person on the Moon as an astronaut within the meaning of article V of the Treaty on Principles Governing the Activities of States in the Exploration and Use of

Outer Space, including the Moon and Other Celestial Bodies and as part of the personnel of a spacecraft within the meaning of the Agreement on the Rescue of Astronauts, the Return of Astronauts and the Return of Objects Launched into Outer Space.

2. States Parties shall offer shelter in their stations, installations, vehicles and other facilities to persons in distress on the Moon.

Article 11

1. The Moon and its natural resources are the common heritage of mankind, which finds its expression in the provisions of this Agreement, in particular in paragraph 5 of this article.

2. The Moon is not subject to national appropriation by any claim of sovereignty, by means of use or occupation, or by any other means.

3. Neither the surface nor the subsurface of the Moon, nor any part thereof or natural resources in place, shall become property of any State, international intergovernmental or non-governmental organization, national organization or non-governmental entity or of any natural person. The placement of personnel, space vehicles, equipment, facilities, stations and installations on or below the surface of the Moon, including structures connected with its surface or subsurface, shall not create a right of ownership over the surface or the subsurface of the Moon or any areas thereof. The foregoing provisions are without prejudice to the international regime referred to in paragraph 5 of this article.

4. States Parties have the right to exploration and use of the Moon without discrimination of any kind, on the basis of equality and in accordance with international law and the terms of this Agreement.

5. States Parties to this Agreement hereby undertake to establish an international regime, including appropriate procedures, to govern the exploitation of the natural resources of the Moon as such exploitation is about to become feasible. This provision shall be implemented in accordance with article 18 of this Agreement.

6. In order to facilitate the establishment of the international regime referred to in paragraph 5 of this article, States Parties shall inform the Secretary-General of the United Nations as well as the public and the international scientific community, to the greatest extent feasible and practicable, of any natural resources they may discover on the Moon.

7. The main purposes of the international regime to be established shall include:

   (a) The orderly and safe development of the natural resources of the Moon;

(b) The rational management of those resources;

(c) The expansion of opportunities in the use of those resources;

(d) An equitable sharing by all States Parties in the benefits derived from those resources, whereby the interests and needs of the developing countries, as well as the efforts of those countries which have contributed either directly or indirectly to the exploration of the Moon, shall be given special consideration.

8. All the activities with respect to the natural resources of the Moon shall be carried out in a manner compatible with the purposes specified in paragraph 7 of this article and the provisions of article 6, paragraph 2, of this Agreement.

Article 12

1. States Parties shall retain jurisdiction and control over their personnel, vehicles, equipment, facilities, stations and installations on the Moon. The ownership of space vehicles, equipment, facilities, stations and installations shall not be affected by their presence on the Moon.
2. Vehicles, installations and equipment or their component parts found in places other than their intended location shall be dealt with in accordance with article 5 of the Agreement on the Rescue of Astronauts, the Return of Astronauts and the Return of Objects Launched into Outer Space.

3. In the event of an emergency involving a threat to human life, States Parties may use the equipment, vehicles, installations, facilities or supplies of other States Parties on the Moon. Prompt notification of such use shall be made to the Secretary-General of the United Nations or the State Party concerned.

Article 13

A State Party which learns of the crash landing, forced landing or other unintended landing on the Moon of a space object, or its component parts, that were not launched by it, shall promptly inform the launching State Party and the Secretary-General of the United Nations.

Article 14

1. States Parties to this Agreement shall bear international responsibility for national activities on the Moon, whether such activities are carried on by governmental agencies or by non-governmental entities, and for assuring that

national activities are carried out in conformity with the provisions set forth in this Agreement. States Parties shall ensure that non-governmental entities under their jurisdiction shall engage in activities on the Moon only under the authority and continuing supervision of the appropriate State Party.

2. States Parties recognize that detailed arrangements concerning liability for damage caused on the Moon, in addition to the provisions of the Treaty on Principles Governing the Activities of States in the Exploration and Use of Outer Space, including the Moon and Other Celestial Bodies and the Convention on International Liability for Damage Caused by Space Objects, may become necessary as a result of more extensive activities on the Moon. Any such arrangements shall be elaborated in accordance with the procedure provided for in article 18 of this Agreement.

Article 15

1. Each State Party may assure itself that the activities of other States Parties in the exploration and use of the Moon are compatible with the provisions of this Agreement. To this end, all space vehicles, equipment, facilities, stations and installations on the Moon shall be open to other States Parties. Such States Parties shall give reasonable advance notice of a projected visit, in order that appropriate consultations may be held and that maximum precautions may be taken to assure safety and to avoid interference with normal operations in the facility to be visited. In pursuance of this article, any State Party may act on its own behalf or with the full or partial assistance of any other State Party or through appropriate international procedures within the framework of the United Nations and in accordance with the Charter.

2. A State Party which has reason to believe that another State Party is not fulfilling the obligations incumbent upon it pursuant to this Agreement or that another State Party is interfering with the rights which the former State has under this Agreement may request consultations with that State Party. A State Party receiving such a request shall enter into such consultations without delay. Any other State Party which requests to do so shall be entitled to take part in the consultations. Each State Party participating in such consultations shall seek a mutually acceptable resolution of any controversy and shall bear in mind the rights and interests of all States Parties. The Secretary-General of the United Nations shall be informed of the results of the consultations and shall transmit the information received to all States Parties concerned.

3. If the consultations do not lead to a mutually acceptable settlement which has due regard for the rights and interests of all States Parties, the parties concerned shall take all measures to settle the dispute by other peaceful means of their choice appropriate to the circumstances and the nature of the dispute.

If difficulties arise in connection with the opening of consultations or if consultations do not lead to a mutually acceptable settlement, any State Party may seek the assistance of the Secretary-General, without seeking the consent of any other State Party concerned, in order to resolve the controversy. A State Party which does not maintain diplomatic relations with another State Party concerned shall participate in such consultations, at its choice, either itself or through another State Party or the Secretary-General as intermediary.

Article 16

With the exception of articles 17 to 21, references in this Agreement to States shall be deemed to apply to any international intergovernmental organization which conducts space activities if the organization declares its acceptance of the rights and obligations provided for in this Agreement and if a majority of the States members of the organization are States Parties to this Agreement and to the Treaty on Principles Governing the Activities of States in the Exploration and Use of Outer Space, including the Moon and Other Celestial Bodies. States members of any such organization which are States Parties to this Agreement shall take all appropriate steps to ensure that the organization makes a declaration in accordance with the foregoing.

Article 17

Any State Party to this Agreement may propose amendments to the Agreement. Amendments shall enter into force for each State Party to the Agreement accepting the amendments upon their acceptance by a majority of the States Parties to the Agreement and thereafter for each remaining State Party to the Agreement on the date of acceptance by it.

Article 18

Ten years after the entry into force of this Agreement, the question of the review of the Agreement shall be included in the provisional agenda of the General Assembly of the United Nations in order to consider, in the light of past application of the Agreement, whether it requires revision. However, at any time after the Agreement has been in force for five years, the Secretary-General of the United Nations, as depositary, shall, at the request of one third of the States Parties to the Agreement and with the concurrence of the majority of the States Parties, convene a conference of the States Parties to review this Agreement. A review conference shall also consider the question of the implementation of the provisions of article 11, paragraph 5, on the basis of the principle referred to in paragraph 1 of that article and taking into account in particular any relevant technological developments.

Article 19

1. This Agreement shall be open for signature by all States at United Nations Headquarters in New York.

2. This Agreement shall be subject to ratification by signatory States. Any State which does not sign this Agreement before its entry into force in accordance with paragraph 3 of this article may accede to it at any time. Instruments of ratification or accession shall be deposited with the Secretary-General of the United Nations.

3. This Agreement shall enter into force on the thirtieth day following the date of deposit of the fifth instrument of ratification.

4. For each State depositing its instrument of ratification or accession after the entry into force of this Agreement, it shall enter into force on the thirtieth day following the date of deposit of any such instrument.

5. The Secretary-General shall promptly inform all signatory and acceding States of the date of each signature, the date of deposit of each instrument of ratification or accession to this Agreement, the date of its entry into force and other notices.

Article 20

Any State Party to this Agreement may give notice of its withdrawal from the Agreement one year after its entry into force by written notification to the Secretary-General of the United Nations. Such withdrawal shall take effect one year from the date of receipt of this notification.

Article 21

The original of this Agreement, of which the Arabic, Chinese, English, French, Russian and Spanish texts are equally authentic, shall be deposited with the Secretary-General of the United Nations, who shall send certified copies thereof to all signatory and acceding States.

IN WITNESS WHEREOF the undersigned, being duly authorized thereto by their respective Governments, have signed this Agreement, opened for signature at New York on the eighteenth day of December, one thousand nine hundred and seventy-nine.

F. United Nations treaties depositary information

1. 1967 Treaty on Principles Governing the Activities of States in the Exploration and Use of Outer Space, including the Moon and Other Celestial Bodies (Outer Space Treaty)

   Adoption by the General Assembly on 19 December 1966 under resolution 2222 (XXI)

   Opened for signature on 27 January 1967 in London, Moscow and Washington, D.C.

   Entry into force on 10 October 1967

   Depositaries: Russian Federation, United Kingdom of Great Britain and Northern Ireland and United States of America

2. 1968 Agreement on the Rescue of Astronauts, the Return of Astronauts and the Return of Objects Launched into Outer Space (Rescue Agreement)

   Adoption by the General Assembly on 19 December 1967 under resolution 2345 (XXII)

   Opened for signature on 22 April 1968 in London, Moscow and Washington, D.C.

   Entry into force on 3 December 1968

   Depositaries: Russian Federation, United Kingdom of Great Britain and Northern Ireland and United States of America

3. 1972 Convention on International Liability for Damage Caused by Space Objects (Liability Convention)

   Adoption by the General Assembly on 29 November 1971 under resolution 2777 (XXVI)

   Opened for signature on 29 March 1972 in London, Moscow and Washington, D.C.

   Entry into force on 1 September 1972

   Depositaries: Russian Federation, United Kingdom of Great Britain and Northern Ireland and United States of America

4. 1975 Convention on Registration of Objects Launched into Outer Space (Registration Convention)

   Adoption by the General Assembly on 12 November 1974 under resolution 3235 (XXIX)

   Opened for signature on 14 January 1975 in New York

   Entry into force on 15 September 1976

   Depositary: Secretary-General of the United Nations

5. 1979 Agreement Governing the Activities of States on the Moon and Other Celestial Bodies

   Adoption by the General Assembly on 5 December 1979 under resolution 34/68

   Opened for signature on 18 December 1979 in New York

   Entry into force on 11 July 1984

   Depositary: Secretary-General of the United Nations

Part two

Principles adopted by the General Assembly

A. Declaration of Legal Principles Governing the Activities of States in the Exploration and Use of Outer Space[7]

The General Assembly,

Inspired by the great prospects opening up before mankind as a result of man's entry into outer space,

Recognizing the common interest of all mankind in the progress of the exploration and use of outer space for peaceful purposes,

Believing that the exploration and use of outer space should be carried on for the betterment of mankind and for the benefit of States irrespective of their degree of economic or scientific development,

Desiring to contribute to broad international cooperation in the scientific as well as in the legal aspects of exploration and use of outer space for peaceful purposes,

Believing that such cooperation will contribute to the development of mutual understanding and to the strengthening of friendly relations between nations and peoples,

Recalling its resolution 110 (II) of 3 November 1947, which condemned propaganda designed or likely to provoke or encourage any threat to the peace, breach of the peace, or act of aggression, and considering that the aforementioned resolution is applicable to outer space,

Taking into consideration its resolutions 1721 (XVI) of 20 December 1961 and 1802 (XVII) of 14 December 1962, adopted unanimously by the States Members of the United Nations,

Solemnly declares that in the exploration and use of outer space States should be guided by the following principles:

---

[7]Adopted by the General Assembly in its resolution 1962 (XVIII) of 13 December 1963.

1. The exploration and use of outer space shall be carried on for the benefit and in the interests of all mankind.

2. Outer space and celestial bodies are free for exploration and use by all States on a basis of equality and in accordance with international law.

3. Outer space and celestial bodies are not subject to national appropriation by claim of sovereignty, by means of use or occupation, or by any other means.

4. The activities of States in the exploration and use of outer space shall be carried on in accordance with international law, including the Charter of the United Nations, in the interest of maintaining international peace and security and promoting international cooperation and understanding.

5. States bear international responsibility for national activities in outer space, whether carried on by governmental agencies or by non-governmental entities, and for assuring that national activities are carried on in conformity with the principles set forth in the present Declaration. The activities of non-governmental entities in outer space shall require authorization and continuing supervision by the State concerned. When activities are carried on in outer space by an international organization, responsibility for compliance with the principles set forth in this Declaration shall be borne by the international organization and by the States participating in it.

6. In the exploration and use of outer space, States shall be guided by the principle of cooperation and mutual assistance and shall conduct all their activities in outer space with due regard for the corresponding interests of other States. If a State has reason to believe that an outer space activity or experiment planned by it or its nationals would cause potentially harmful interference with activities of other States in the peaceful exploration and use of outer space, it shall undertake appropriate international consultations before proceeding with any such activity or experiment. A State which has reason to believe that an outer space activity or experiment planned by another State would cause potentially harmful interference with activities in the peaceful exploration and use of outer space may request consultation concerning the activity or experiment.

7. The State on whose registry an object launched into outer space is carried shall retain jurisdiction and control over such object, and any personnel thereon, while in outer space. Ownership of objects launched into outer space, and of their component parts, is not affected by their passage through outer space or by their return to the Earth. Such objects or component parts found beyond the limits of the State of registry shall be returned to that State, which shall furnish identifying data upon request prior to return.

8. Each State which launches or procures the launching of an object into outer space, and each State from whose territory or facility an object is launched,

is internationally liable for damage to a foreign State or to its natural or juridical persons by such object or its component parts on the Earth, in air space, or in outer space.

9. States shall regard astronauts as envoys of mankind in outer space, and shall render to them all possible assistance in the event of accident, distress, or emergency landing on the territory of a foreign State or on the high seas. Astronauts who make such a landing shall be safely and promptly returned to the State of registry of their space vehicle.

B. Principles Governing the Use by States of Artificial Earth Satellites for International Direct Television Broadcasting[8]

The General Assembly,

Recalling its resolution 2916 (XXVII) of 9 November 1972, in which it stressed the necessity of elaborating principles governing the use by States of artificial Earth satellites for international direct television broadcasting, and mindful of the importance of concluding an international agreement or agreements,

Recalling further its resolutions 3182 (XXVIII) of 18 December 1973, 3234 (XXIX) of 12 November 1974, 3388 (XXX) of 18 November 1975, 31/8 of 8 November 1976, 32/196 of 20 December 1977, 33/16 of 10 November 1978, 34/66 of 5 December 1979 and 35/14 of 3 November 1980, and its resolution 36/35 of 18 November 1981 in which it decided to consider at its thirty-seventh session the adoption of a draft set of principles governing the use by States of artificial Earth satellites for international direct television broadcasting,

Noting with appreciation the efforts made in the Committee on the Peaceful Uses of Outer Space and its Legal Subcommittee to comply with the directives issued in the above-mentioned resolutions,

Considering that several experiments of direct broadcasting by satellite have been carried out and that a number of direct broadcasting satellite systems are operational in some countries and may be commercialized in the very near future,

Taking into consideration that the operation of international direct broadcasting satellites will have significant international political, economic, social and cultural implications,

Believing that the establishment of principles for international direct television broadcasting will contribute to the strengthening of international

[8]Adopted by the General Assembly in its resolution 37/92 of 10 December 1982.

cooperation in this field and further the purposes and principles of the Charter of the United Nations,

Adopts the Principles Governing the Use by States of Artificial Earth Satellites for International Direct Television Broadcasting set forth in the annex to the present resolution.

Annex. Principles Governing the Use by States of Artificial Earth Satellites for International Direct Television Broadcasting

A. *Purposes and objectives*

1. Activities in the field of international direct television broadcasting by satellite should be carried out in a manner compatible with the sovereign rights of States, including the principle of non-intervention, as well as with the right of everyone to seek, receive and impart information and ideas as enshrined in the relevant United Nations instruments.

2. Such activities should promote the free dissemination and mutual exchange of information and knowledge in cultural and scientific fields, assist in educational, social and economic development, particularly in the developing countries, enhance the qualities of life of all peoples and provide recreation with due respect to the political and cultural integrity of States.

3. These activities should accordingly be carried out in a manner compatible with the development of mutual understanding and the strengthening of friendly relations and cooperation among all States and peoples in the interest of maintaining international peace and security.

B. *Applicability of international law*

4. Activities in the field of international direct television broadcasting by satellite should be conducted in accordance with international law, including the Charter of the United Nations, the Treaty on Principles Governing the Activities of States in the Exploration and Use of Outer Space, including the Moon and Other Celestial Bodies,[1] of 27 January 1967, the relevant provisions of the International Telecommunication Convention and its Radio Regulations and of international instruments relating to friendly relations and cooperation among States and to human rights.

C. *Rights and benefits*

5. Every State has an equal right to conduct activities in the field of international direct television broadcasting by satellite and to authorize such

activities by persons and entities under its jurisdiction. All States and peoples are entitled to and should enjoy the benefits from such activities. Access to the technology in this field should be available to all States without discrimination on terms mutually agreed by all concerned.

D. *International cooperation*

6. Activities in the field of international direct television broadcasting by satellite should be based upon and encourage international cooperation. Such cooperation should be the subject of appropriate arrangements. Special consideration should be given to the needs of the developing countries in the use of international direct television broadcasting by satellite for the purpose of accelerating their national development.

E. *Peaceful settlement of disputes*

7. Any international dispute that may arise from activities covered by these principles should be settled through established procedures for the peaceful settlement of disputes agreed upon by the parties to the dispute in accordance with the provisions of the Charter of the United Nations.

F. *State responsibility*

8. States should bear international responsibility for activities in the field of international direct television broadcasting by satellite carried out by them or under their jurisdiction and for the conformity of any such activities with the principles set forth in this document.

9. When international direct television broadcasting by satellite is carried out by an international intergovernmental organization, the responsibility referred to in paragraph 8 above should be borne both by that organization and by the States participating in it.

G. *Duty and right to consult*

10. Any broadcasting or receiving State within an international direct television broadcasting satellite service established between them requested to do so by any other broadcasting or receiving State within the same service should promptly enter into consultations with the requesting State regarding its activities in the field of international direct television broadcasting by satellite, without prejudice to other consultations which these States may undertake with any other State on that subject.

H. Copyright and neighbouring rights

11. Without prejudice to the relevant provisions of international law, States should cooperate on a bilateral and multilateral basis for protection of copyright and neighbouring rights by means of appropriate agreements between the interested States or the competent legal entities acting under their jurisdiction. In such cooperation they should give special consideration to the interests of developing countries in the use of direct television broadcasting for the purpose of accelerating their national development.

I. Notification to the United Nations

12. In order to promote international cooperation in the peaceful exploration and use of outer space, States conducting or authorizing activities in the field of international direct television broadcasting by satellite should inform the Secretary-General of the United Nations, to the greatest extent possible, of the nature of such activities. On receiving this information, the Secretary-General should disseminate it immediately and effectively to the relevant specialized agencies, as well as to the public and the international scientific community.

J. Consultations and agreements between States

13. A State which intends to establish or authorize the establishment of an international direct television broadcasting satellite service shall without delay notify the proposed receiving State or States of such intention and shall promptly enter into consultation with any of those States which so requests.

14. An international direct television broadcasting satellite service shall only be established after the conditions set forth in paragraph 13 above have been met and on the basis of agreements and/or arrangements in conformity with the relevant instruments of the International Telecommunication Union and in accordance with these principles.

15. With respect to the unavoidable overspill of the radiation of the satellite signal, the relevant instruments of the International Telecommunication Union shall be exclusively applicable.

C. Principles Relating to Remote Sensing of the Earth from Outer Space[9]

The General Assembly,

Recalling its resolution 3234 (XXIX) of 12 November 1974, in which it recommended that the Legal Subcommittee of the Committee on the Peaceful Uses of Outer Space should consider the question of the legal implications of remote sensing of the Earth from space, as well as its resolutions 3388 (XXX) of 18 November 1975, 31/8 of 8 November 1976, 32/196 A of 20 December 1977, 33/16 of 10 November 1978, 34/66 of 5 December 1979, 35/14 of 3 November 1980, 36/35 of 18 November 1981, 37/89 of 10 December 1982, 38/80 of 15 December 1983, 39/96 of 14 December 1984 and 40/162 of 16 December 1985, in which it called for a detailed consideration of the legal implications of remote sensing of the Earth from space, with the aim of formulating draft principles relating to remote sensing,

Having considered the report of the Committee on the Peaceful Uses of Outer Space on the work of its twenty-ninth session[10] and the text of the draft principles relating to remote sensing of the Earth from space, annexed thereto,

Noting with satisfaction that the Committee on the Peaceful Uses of Outer Space, on the basis of the deliberations of its Legal Subcommittee, has endorsed the text of the draft principles relating to remote sensing of the Earth from space,

Believing that the adoption of the principles relating to remote sensing of the Earth from space will contribute to the strengthening of international cooperation in this field,

Adopts the principles relating to remote sensing of the Earth from space set forth in the annex to the present resolution.

---

[9]Adopted by the General Assembly in its resolution 41/65 of 3 December 1986.

[10]*Official Records of the General Assembly, Forty-first Session, Supplement No. 20* and corrigendum (A/41/20 and Corr.1).

Annex. Principles Relating to Remote Sensing of the Earth from Outer Space

Principle I

For the purposes of these principles with respect to remote sensing activities:

(a) The term "remote sensing" means the sensing of the Earth's surface from space by making use of the properties of electromagnetic waves emitted, reflected or diffracted by the sensed objects, for the purpose of improving natural resources management, land use and the protection of the environment;

(b) The term "primary data" means those raw data that are acquired by remote sensors borne by a space object and that are transmitted or delivered to the ground from space by telemetry in the form of electromagnetic signals, by photographic film, magnetic tape or any other means;

(c) The term "processed data" means the products resulting from the processing of the primary data, needed to make such data usable;

(d) The term "analysed information" means the information resulting from the interpretation of processed data, inputs of data and knowledge from other sources;

(e) The term "remote sensing activities" means the operation of remote sensing space systems, primary data collection and storage stations, and activities in processing, interpreting and disseminating the processed data.

Principle II

Remote sensing activities shall be carried out for the benefit and in the interests of all countries, irrespective of their degree of economic, social or scientific and technological development, and taking into particular consideration the needs of the developing countries.

Principle III

Remote sensing activities shall be conducted in accordance with international law, including the Charter of the United Nations, the Treaty on Principles Governing the Activities of States in the Exploration and Use of Outer Space, including the Moon and Other Celestial Bodies,[1] and the relevant instruments of the International Telecommunication Union.

Principle IV

Remote sensing activities shall be conducted in accordance with the principles contained in article I of the Treaty on Principles Governing the Activities of States in the Exploration and Use of Outer Space, including the Moon and Other Celestial Bodies, which, in particular, provides that the exploration and use of outer space shall be carried out for the benefit and in the interests of all countries, irrespective of their degree of economic or scientific development, and stipulates the principle of freedom of exploration and use of outer space on the basis of equality. These activities shall be conducted on the basis of respect for the principle of full and permanent sovereignty of all States and peoples over their own wealth and natural resources, with due regard to the rights and interests, in accordance with international law, of other States and entities under their jurisdiction. Such activities shall not be conducted in a manner detrimental to the legitimate rights and interests of the sensed State.

Principle V

States carrying out remote sensing activities shall promote international cooperation in these activities. To this end, they shall make available to other States opportunities for participation therein. Such participation shall be based in each case on equitable and mutually acceptable terms.

Principle VI

In order to maximize the availability of benefits from remote sensing activities, States are encouraged, through agreements or other arrangements, to provide for the establishment and operation of data collecting and storage stations and processing and interpretation facilities, in particular within the framework of regional agreements or arrangements wherever feasible.

Principle VII

States participating in remote sensing activities shall make available technical assistance to other interested States on mutually agreed terms.

Principle VIII

The United Nations and the relevant agencies within the United Nations system shall promote international cooperation, including technical assistance and coordination in the area of remote sensing.

Principle IX

In accordance with article IV of the Convention on Registration of Objects Launched into Outer Space4 and article XI of the Treaty on Principles Governing the Activities of States in the Exploration and Use of Outer Space, including the Moon and Other Celestial Bodies, a State carrying out a programme of remote sensing shall inform the Secretary-General of the United Nations. It shall, moreover, make available any other relevant information to the greatest extent feasible and practicable to any other State, particularly any developing country that is affected by the programme, at its request.

Principle X

Remote sensing shall promote the protection of the Earth's natural environment.

To this end, States participating in remote sensing activities that have identified information in their possession that is capable of averting any phenomenon harmful to the Earth's natural environment shall disclose such information to States concerned.

Principle XI

Remote sensing shall promote the protection of mankind from natural disasters.

To this end, States participating in remote sensing activities that have identified processed data and analysed information in their possession that may be useful to States affected by natural disasters, or likely to be affected by impending natural disasters, shall transmit such data and information to States concerned as promptly as possible.

Principle XII

As soon as the primary data and the processed data concerning the territory under its jurisdiction are produced, the sensed State shall have access to them on a non-discriminatory basis and on reasonable cost terms. The sensed State shall also have access to the available analysed information concerning the territory under its jurisdiction in the possession of any State participating in remote sensing activities on the same basis and terms, taking particularly into account the needs and interests of the developing countries.

Principle XIII

To promote and intensify international cooperation, especially with regard to the needs of developing countries, a State carrying out remote sensing of the Earth from space shall, upon request, enter into consultations with a State whose territory is sensed in order to make available opportunities for participation and enhance the mutual benefits to be derived therefrom.

Principle XIV

In compliance with article VI of the Treaty on Principles Governing the Activities of States in the Exploration and Use of Outer Space, including the Moon and Other Celestial Bodies, States operating remote sensing satellites shall bear international responsibility for their activities and assure that such activities are conducted in accordance with these principles and the norms of international law, irrespective of whether such activities are carried out by governmental or non-governmental entities or through international organizations to which such States are parties. This principle is without prejudice to the applicability of the norms of international law on State responsibility for remote sensing activities.

Principle XV

Any dispute resulting from the application of these principles shall be resolved through the established procedures for the peaceful settlement of disputes.

D. Principles Relevant to the Use of Nuclear Power Sources in Outer Space[11]

The General Assembly,

Having considered the report of the Committee on the Peaceful Uses of Outer Space on the work of its thirty-fifth session[12] and the text of the Principles Relevant to the Use of Nuclear Power Sources in Outer Space as approved by the Committee and annexed to its report,[13]

Recognizing that for some missions in outer space nuclear power sources are particularly suited or even essential owing to their compactness, long life and other attributes,

Recognizing also that the use of nuclear power sources in outer space should focus on those applications which take advantage of the particular properties of nuclear power sources,

Recognizing further that the use of nuclear power sources in outer space should be based on a thorough safety assessment, including probabilistic risk analysis, with particular emphasis on reducing the risk of accidental exposure of the public to harmful radiation or radioactive material,

Recognizing the need, in this respect, for a set of principles containing goals and guidelines to ensure the safe use of nuclear power sources in outer space,

Affirming that this set of Principles applies to nuclear power sources in outer space devoted to the generation of electric power on board space objects for nonpropulsive purposes, which have characteristics generally comparable to those of systems used and missions performed at the time of the adoption of the Principles,

Recognizing that this set of Principles will require future revision in view of emerging nuclear power applications and of evolving international recommendations on radiological protection,

Adopts the Principles Relevant to the Use of Nuclear Power Sources in Outer Space as set forth below.

---

[11]Adopted by the General Assembly in its resolution 47/68 of 14 December 1992.

[12]*Official Records of the General Assembly, Forty-seventh Session, Supplement No. 20* (A/47/20).

[13]Ibid., annex.

Principle 1. Applicability of international law

Activities involving the use of nuclear power sources in outer space shall be carried out in accordance with international law, including in particular the Charter of the United Nations and the Treaty on Principles Governing the Activities of States in the Exploration and Use of Outer Space, including the Moon and Other Celestial Bodies.[1]

Principle 2. Use of terms

1. For the purpose of these Principles, the terms "launching State" and "State launching" mean the State which exercises jurisdiction and control over a space object with nuclear power sources on board at a given point in time relevant to the principle concerned.

2. For the purpose of principle 9, the definition of the term "launching State" as contained in that principle is applicable.

3. For the purposes of principle 3, the terms "foreseeable" and "all possible" describe a class of events or circumstances whose overall probability of occurrence is such that it is considered to encompass only credible possibilities for purposes of safety analysis. The term "general concept of defence-in-depth" when applied to nuclear power sources in outer space refers to the use of design features and mission operations in place of or in addition to active systems, to prevent or mitigate the consequences of system malfunctions. Redundant safety systems are not necessarily required for each individual component to achieve this purpose. Given the special requirements of space use and of varied missions, no particular set of systems or features can be specified as essential to achieve this objective. For the purposes of paragraph 2 *(d)* of principle 3, the term "made critical" does not include actions such as zero-power testing which are fundamental to ensuring system safety.

Principle 3. Guidelines and criteria for safe use

In order to minimize the quantity of radioactive material in space and the risks involved, the use of nuclear power sources in outer space shall be restricted to those space missions which cannot be operated by non-nuclear energy sources in a reasonable way.

1. General goals for radiation protection and nuclear safety

(a) States launching space objects with nuclear power sources on board shall endeavour to protect individuals, populations and the biosphere against

radiological hazards. The design and use of space objects with nuclear power sources on board shall ensure, with a high degree of confidence, that the hazards, in foreseeable operational or accidental circumstances, are kept below acceptable levels as defined in paragraphs 1 *(b)* and *(c).*

Such design and use shall also ensure with high reliability that radioactive material does not cause a significant contamination of outer space;

(b) During the normal operation of space objects with nuclear power sources on board, including re-entry from the sufficiently high orbit as defined in paragraph 2 *(b),* the appropriate radiation protection objective for the public recommended by the International Commission on Radiological Protection shall be observed. During such normal operation there shall be no significant radiation exposure;

(c) To limit exposure in accidents, the design and construction of the nuclear power source systems shall take into account relevant and generally accepted international radiological protection guidelines.

Except in cases of low-probability accidents with potentially serious radiological consequences, the design for the nuclear power source systems shall, with a high degree of confidence, restrict radiation exposure to a limited geographical region and to individuals to the principal limit of 1 mSv in a year. It is permissible to use a subsidiary dose limit of 5 mSv in a year for some years, provided that the average annual effective dose equivalent over a lifetime does not exceed the principal limit of 1 mSv in a year.

The probability of accidents with potentially serious radiological consequences referred to above shall be kept extremely small by virtue of the design of the system.

Future modifications of the guidelines referred to in this paragraph shall be applied as soon as practicable;

(d) Systems important for safety shall be designed, constructed and operated in accordance with the general concept of defence-in-depth. Pursuant to this concept, foreseeable safety-related failures or malfunctions must be capable of being corrected or counteracted by an action or a procedure, possibly automatic.

The reliability of systems important for safety shall be ensured, inter alia, by redundancy, physical separation, functional isolation and adequate independence of their components.

Other measures shall also be taken to raise the level of safety.

2. *Nuclear reactors*

(a) Nuclear reactors may be operated:

(i) On interplanetary missions;

(ii) In sufficiently high orbits as defined in paragraph 2 *(b);*

(iii) In low-Earth orbits if they are stored in sufficiently high orbits after the operational part of their mission.

(b) The sufficiently high orbit is one in which the orbital lifetime is long enough to allow for a sufficient decay of the fission products to approximately the activity of the actinides. The sufficiently high orbit must be such that the risks to existing and future outer space missions and of collision with other space objects are kept to a minimum. The necessity for the parts of a destroyed reactor also to attain the required decay time before re-entering the Earth's atmosphere shall be considered in determining the sufficiently high orbit altitude;

(c) Nuclear reactors shall use only highly enriched uranium 235 as fuel. The design shall take into account the radioactive decay of the fission and activation products;

(d) Nuclear reactors shall not be made critical before they have reached their operating orbit or interplanetary trajectory;

(e) The design and construction of the nuclear reactor shall ensure that it cannot become critical before reaching the operating orbit during all possible events, including rocket explosion, re-entry, impact on ground or water, submersion in water or water intruding into the core;

(f) In order to reduce significantly the possibility of failures in satellites with nuclear reactors on board during operations in an orbit with a lifetime less than in the sufficiently high orbit (including operations for transfer into the sufficiently high orbit), there shall be a highly reliable operational system to ensure an effective and controlled disposal of the reactor.

3. *Radioisotope generators*

(a) Radioisotope generators may be used for interplanetary missions and other missions leaving the gravity field of the Earth. They may also be used in Earth orbit if, after conclusion of the operational part of their mission, they are stored in a high orbit. In any case ultimate disposal is necessary;

(b) Radioisotope generators shall be protected by a containment system that is designed and constructed to withstand the heat and aerodynamic forces of re-entry in the upper atmosphere under foreseeable orbital conditions,

including highly elliptical or hyperbolic orbits where relevant. Upon impact, the containment system and the physical form of the isotope shall ensure that no radioactive material is scattered into the environment so that the impact area can be completely cleared of radioactivity by a recovery operation.

Principle 4. Safety assessment

1. A launching State as defined in principle 2, paragraph 1, at the time of launch shall, prior to the launch, through cooperative arrangements, where relevant, with those which have designed, constructed or manufactured the nuclear power sources, or will operate the space object, or from whose territory or facility such an object will be launched, ensure that a thorough and comprehensive safety assessment is conducted. This assessment shall cover as well all relevant phases of the mission and shall deal with all systems involved, including the means of launching, the space platform, the nuclear power source and its equipment and the means of control and communication between ground and space.

2. This assessment shall respect the guidelines and criteria for safe use contained in principle 3.

3. Pursuant to article XI of the Treaty on Principles Governing the Activities of States in the Exploration and Use of Outer Space, including the Moon and Other Celestial Bodies, the results of this safety assessment, together with, to the extent feasible, an indication of the approximate intended time-frame of the launch, shall be made publicly available prior to each launch, and the Secretary-General of the United Nations shall be informed on how States may obtain such results of the safety assessment as soon as possible prior to each launch.

Principle 5. Notification of re-entry

1. Any State launching a space object with nuclear power sources on board shall in a timely fashion inform States concerned in the event this space object is malfunctioning with a risk of re-entry of radioactive materials to the Earth. The information shall be in accordance with the following format:

(a) *System parameters:*

- (i) Name of launching State or States, including the address of the authority which may be contacted for additional information or assistance in case of accident;
- (ii) International designation;
- (iii) Date and territory or location of launch;

(iv) Information required for best prediction of orbit lifetime, trajectory and impact region;

(v) General function of spacecraft;

(b) *Information on the radiological risk of nuclear power source(s):*

(i) Type of nuclear power source: radioisotopic/reactor;

(ii) The probable physical form, amount and general radiological characteristics of the fuel and contaminated and/or activated components likely to reach the ground. The term "fuel" refers to the nuclear material used as the source of heat or power.

This information shall also be transmitted to the Secretary-General of the United Nations.

2. The information, in accordance with the format above, shall be provided by the launching State as soon as the malfunction has become known. It shall be updated as frequently as practicable and the frequency of dissemination of the updated information shall increase as the anticipated time of re-entry into the dense layers of the Earth's atmosphere approaches so that the international community will be informed of the situation and will have sufficient time to plan for any national response activities deemed necessary.

3. The updated information shall also be transmitted to the Secretary-General of the United Nations with the same frequency.

Principle 6. Consultations

States providing information in accordance with principle 5 shall, as far as reasonably practicable, respond promptly to requests for further information or consultations sought by other States.

Principle 7. Assistance to States

1. Upon the notification of an expected re-entry into the Earth's atmosphere of a space object containing a nuclear power source on board and its components, all States possessing space monitoring and tracking facilities, in the spirit of international cooperation, shall communicate the relevant information that they may have available on the malfunctioning space object with a nuclear power source on board to the Secretary-General of the United Nations and the State concerned as promptly as possible to allow States that might be affected to assess the situation and take any precautionary measures deemed necessary.

2. After re-entry into the Earth's atmosphere of a space object containing a nuclear power source on board and its components:

(a) The launching State shall promptly offer and, if requested by the affected State, provide promptly the necessary assistance to eliminate actual and possible harmful effects, including assistance to identify the location of the area of impact of the nuclear power source on the Earth's surface, to detect the re-entered material and to carry out retrieval or clean-up operations;

(b) All States, other than the launching State, with relevant technical capabilities and international organizations with such technical capabilities shall, to the extent possible, provide necessary assistance upon request by an affected State.

In providing the assistance in accordance with subparagraphs *(a)* and *(b)* above, the special needs of developing countries shall be taken into account.

Principle 8. Responsibility

In accordance with article VI of the Treaty on Principles Governing the Activities of States in the Exploration and Use of Outer Space, including the Moon and Other Celestial Bodies, States shall bear international responsibility for national activities involving the use of nuclear power sources in outer space, whether such activities are carried on by governmental agencies or by non-governmental entities, and for assuring that such national activities are carried out in conformity with that Treaty and the recommendations contained in these Principles. When activities in outer space involving the use of nuclear power sources are carried on by an international organization, responsibility for compliance with the aforesaid Treaty and the recommendations contained in these Principles shall be borne both by the international organization and by the States participating in it.

Principle 9. Liability and compensation

1. In accordance with article VII of the Treaty on Principles Governing the Activities of States in the Exploration and Use of Outer Space, including the Moon and Other Celestial Bodies, and the provisions of the Convention on International Liability for Damage Caused by Space Objects,[3] each State which launches or procures the launching of a space object and each State from whose territory or facility a space object is launched shall be internationally liable for damage caused by such space objects or their component parts. This fully applies to the case of such a space object carrying a nuclear power source on board. Whenever two or more States jointly launch such a space object, they

shall be jointly and severally liable for any damage caused, in accordance with article V of the above-mentioned Convention.

2. The compensation that such States shall be liable to pay under the aforesaid Convention for damage shall be determined in accordance with international law and the principles of justice and equity, in order to provide such reparation in respect of the damage as will restore the person, natural or juridical, State or international organization on whose behalf a claim is presented to the condition which would have existed if the damage had not occurred.

3. For the purposes of this principle, compensation shall include reimbursement of the duly substantiated expenses for search, recovery and clean-up operations, including expenses for assistance received from third parties.

Principle 10. Settlement of disputes

Any dispute resulting from the application of these Principles shall be resolved through negotiations or other established procedures for the peaceful settlement of disputes, in accordance with the Charter of the United Nations.

Principle 11. Review and revision

These Principles shall be reopened for revision by the Committee on the Peaceful Uses of Outer Space no later than two years after their adoption.

E. Declaration on International Cooperation in the Exploration and Use of Outer Space for the Benefit and in the Interest of All States, Taking into Particular Account the Needs of Developing Countries[14]

The General Assembly,

Having considered the report of the Committee on the Peaceful Uses of Outer Space on the work of its thirty-ninth session[15] and the text of the Declaration on International Cooperation in the Exploration and Use of Outer Space for the Benefit and in the Interest of All States, Taking into Particular Account the Needs of Developing Countries, as approved by the Committee and annexed to its report,[16]

Bearing in mind the relevant provisions of the Charter of the United Nations,

Recalling notably the provisions of the Treaty on the Principles Governing the Activities of States in the Exploration and Use of Outer Space, including the Moon and Other Celestial Bodies,[1]

Recalling also its relevant resolutions relating to activities in outer space,

Bearing in mind the recommendations of the Second United Nations Conference on the Exploration and Peaceful Uses of Outer Space,[17] and of other international conferences relevant in this field,

---

[14]Adopted by the General Assembly in its resolution 51/122 of 13 December 1996.

[15]*Official Records of the General Assembly, Fifty-first Session, Supplement No. 20* (A/51/20).

[16]Ibid., annex IV.

[17]See *Report of the Second United Nations Conference on the Exploration and Peaceful Uses of Outer Space, Vienna, 9-21 August 1982* and corrigenda (A/CONF.101/10 and Corr.1 and 2).

Recognizing the growing scope and significance of international cooperation among States and between States and international organizations in the exploration and use of outer space for peaceful purposes,

Considering experiences gained in international cooperative ventures,

Convinced of the necessity and the significance of further strengthening international cooperation in order to reach a broad and efficient collaboration in this field for the mutual benefit and in the interest of all parties involved,

Desirous of facilitating the application of the principle that the exploration and use of outer space, including the Moon and other celestial bodies, shall be carried out for the benefit and in the interest of all countries, irrespective of their degree of economic or scientific development, and shall be the province of all mankind,

Adopts the Declaration on International Cooperation in the Exploration and Use of Outer Space for the Benefit and in the Interest of All States, Taking into Particular Account the Needs of Developing Countries, set forth in the annex to the present resolution.

Annex. Declaration on International Cooperation in the Exploration and Use of Outer Space for the Benefit and in the Interest of all States, Taking into Particular Account the Needs of Developing Countries

1. International cooperation in the exploration and use of outer space for peaceful purposes (hereafter "international cooperation") shall be conducted in accordance with the provisions of international law, including the Charter of the United Nations and the Treaty on the Principles Governing the Activities of States in the Exploration and Use of Outer Space, including the Moon and Other Celestial Bodies. It shall be carried out for the benefit and in the interest of all States, irrespective of their degree of economic, social or scientific and technological development, and shall be the province of all mankind. Particular account should be taken of the needs of developing countries.

2. States are free to determine all aspects of their participation in international cooperation in the exploration and use of outer space on an equitable and mutually acceptable basis. Contractual terms in such cooperative ventures should be fair and reasonable and they should be in full compliance with the legitimate rights and interests of the parties concerned as, for example, with intellectual property rights.

3. All States, particularly those with relevant space capabilities and with programmes for the exploration and use of outer space, should contribute to

promoting and fostering international cooperation on an equitable and mutually acceptable basis. In this context, particular attention should be given to the benefit for and the interests of developing countries and countries with incipient space programmes stemming from such international cooperation conducted with countries with more advanced space capabilities.

4. International cooperation should be conducted in the modes that are considered most effective and appropriate by the countries concerned, including, inter alia, governmental and non-governmental; commercial and non-commercial; global, multilateral, regional or bilateral; and international cooperation among countries in all levels of development.

5. International cooperation, while taking into particular account the needs of developing countries, should aim, inter alia, at the following goals, considering their need for technical assistance and rational and efficient allocation of financial and technical resources:

(a) Promoting the development of space science and technology and of its applications;

(b) Fostering the development of relevant and appropriate space capabilities in interested States;

(c) Facilitating the exchange of expertise and technology among States on a mutually acceptable basis.

6. National and international agencies, research institutions, organizations for development aid, and developed and developing countries alike should consider the appropriate use of space applications and the potential of international cooperation for reaching their development goals.

7. The Committee on the Peaceful Uses of Outer Space should be strengthened in its role, among others, as a forum for the exchange of information on national and international activities in the field of international cooperation in the exploration and use of outer space.

8. All States should be encouraged to contribute to the United Nations Programme on Space Applications and to other initiatives in the field of international cooperation in accordance with their space capabilities and their participation in the exploration and use of outer space.

Part three

Related resolutions adopted by the General Assembly

A. Resolution 1721 A and B (XVI) of 20 December 1961

International cooperation in the peaceful uses of outer space

A

The General Assembly,

Recognizing the common interest of mankind in furthering the peaceful uses of outer space and the urgent need to strengthen international cooperation in this important field,

Believing that the exploration and use of outer space should be only for the betterment of mankind and to the benefit of States irrespective of the stage of their economic or scientific development,

1. *Commends* to States for their guidance in the exploration and use of outer space the following principles:

(a) International law, including the Charter of the United Nations, applies to outer space and celestial bodies;

(b) Outer space and celestial bodies are free for exploration and use by all States in conformity with international law and are not subject to national appropriation;

2. *Invites* the Committee on the Peaceful Uses of Outer Space to study and report on the legal problems which may arise from the exploration and use of outer space.

B

The General Assembly,

Believing that the United Nations should provide a focal point for international cooperation in the peaceful exploration and use of outer space.

1. *Calls upon* States launching objects into orbit or beyond to furnish information promptly to the Committee on the Peaceful Uses of Outer Space, through the Secretary-General, for the registration of launchings;

2. *Requests* The Secretary-General to maintain a public registry of the information furnished in accordance with paragraph 1 above;

3. *Requests* the Committee on the Peaceful Uses of Outer Space, in cooperation with the Secretary-General and making full use of the functions and resources of the Secretariat:

(a) To maintain close contact with governmental and non-governmental organizations concerned with outer space matters;

(b) To provide for the exchange of such information relating to outer space activities as Governments may supply on a voluntary basis, supplementing but not duplicating existing technical and scientific exchanges;

(c) To assist in the study of measures for the promotion of international cooperation in outer space activities;

4. *Further requests* the Committee on the Peaceful Uses of Outer Space to report to the General Assembly on the arrangements undertaken for the performance of those functions and on such developments relating to the peaceful uses of outer space as it considers significant.

B. Paragraph 4 of resolution 55/122 of 8 December 2000

International cooperation in the peaceful uses of outer space

The General Assembly,

. . .

4. *Notes with satisfaction* the agreement reached by the Legal Subcommittee on the question of the character and utilization of the geostationary orbit and the subsequent endorsement of that agreement by the Committee;[18]

. . .

Some aspects concerning the use of the geostationary orbit

Paper adopted by the Legal Subcommittee at its thirty-ninth session (A/AC.105/738, annex III)

1. In its related resolutions, the General Assembly has regularly endorsed the recommendations of the Committee on the Peaceful Uses of Outer Space that its Legal Subcommittee continue its examination of matters relating to the definition and delimitation of outer space and to the character and utilization of the geostationary orbit, including consideration of ways and means to ensure the rational and equitable use of this orbit, without prejudice to the role of the International Telecommunication Union (ITU).

2. In 1996, Colombia submitted to the Legal Subcommittee at its thirty-fifth session a working paper entitled "Some considerations concerning the utilization of the geostationary orbit" (A/AC.105/C.2/L.200 and Corr.1), recommending certain principles that could be applied to the management of frequencies and orbital positions relating to the geostationary satellite orbit.

[18]See *Official Records of the General Assembly, Fifty-fifth Session, Supplement No. 20 (A/55/20),* para. 129, and A/AC.105/738, annex III.

3. Following the presentation and ensuing discussion, it did not prove possible for the Legal Subcommittee to endorse the paper. At the thirty-eighth session of the Legal Subcommittee, in 1999, after an impressive presentation made by the representative of Colombia, the outcome of the discussion was that Colombia's standpoint should secure agreement on a text that would address the concerns expressed, without leading to implementation difficulties with ITU.

4. The Legal Subcommittee must find a way to reach an agreement on this important question. With this in mind and taking into account all of the points of view that have been expressed, the Legal Subcommittee adopts the recommendations made in paragraph 8 below.

5. Article 44, paragraph 196.2, of the ITU Constitution as amended by the Plenipotentiary Conference, held in Minneapolis, United States of America, in 1998, states:

> "In using frequency bands for radio services, Member States shall bear in mind that radio frequencies and any associated orbits, including the geostationary satellite orbit, are limited natural resources and that they must be used rationally, efficiently and economically, in conformity with the provisions of the Radio Regulations, so that countries or groups of countries may have equitable access to those orbits and frequencies, taking into account the special needs of the developing countries and the geographical situation of particular countries."

6. Access to frequency bands other than those which are planned is at present governed by the principle of "first come, first served". That approach, while suited to developed countries, may disadvantage developing countries, especially those yet to have access to that orbit. The existing coordination procedures that apply to the non-planned bands are designed to overcome that difficulty, but they are not necessarily capable of giving full satisfaction. There is therefore a need to facilitate access to the orbit/spectrum resource by developing countries or countries yet to have access to that orbit/spectrum resource in relation to those already using it, that is, to ensure equitable access between those countries already having access to the orbit/spectrum resource and those seeking it.

7. In conclusion, the Legal Subcommittee considers that:

(a) In accordance with article 44 of the ITU Constitution, the satellite orbits and radio frequency spectrum are limited natural resources, which must be used rationally, efficiently, economically and equitably;

(b) It is necessary to facilitate equitable access to the orbit/spectrum resource;

(c) ITU has planned the use of certain frequency bands and services for the geostationary orbit;

(d) In many frequency bands and services access to frequencies and satellite orbits, including the geostationary satellite orbit, takes place according to the principle of "first come, first served";

(e) The current regulations on access to frequencies and satellite orbits in respect of bands and services may give rise to situations involving difficult processes of coordination among developed as well as developing countries.

8. The Legal Subcommittee therefore recommends that:

(a) Where coordination is required between countries with a view to the utilization of satellite orbits, including the geostationary satellite orbit, the countries concerned take into account the fact that access to that orbit must take place, inter alia, in an equitable manner and according to the ITU Radio Regulations. Consequently, in the case of comparable requests for access to the spectrum/orbit resource by a country already having access to the orbit/spectrum resource and a developing country or another country seeking it, the country already having such access should take all practicable steps to enable the developing country or other country to have equitable access to the requested orbit/spectrum resource;

(b) Countries wishing to use frequencies and satellite orbits, including the geostationary satellite orbit, in the above-mentioned cases file such requests according to the relevant provisions of the ITU Radio Regulations, taking into account resolution 18 of the ITU Plenipotentiary Conference (Kyoto, 1994) and resolution 49 of the ITU World Radiocommunications Conference (Geneva, 1997) in order to guarantee effective use of the orbit/spectrum resource;

(c) Item 6 of the agenda of the Legal Subcommittee continues to remain on the agenda of the Subcommittee. However, no working group shall be convened on the issue of equitable access to the geostationary orbit. This decision could be re-examined in due course, in accordance with the Subcommittee's normal procedure, if further developments warranted;

(d) This document will be made available to ITU.

C. Resolution 59/115 of 10 December 2004

Application of the concept of the "launching State"

The General Assembly,

Recalling the Convention on International Liability for Damage Caused by Space Objects[3] and the Convention on Registration of Objects Launched into Outer Space,[4]

Bearing in mind that the term "launching State" as used in the Liability Convention and the Registration Convention is important in space law, that a launching State shall register a space object in accordance with the Registration Convention and that the Liability Convention identifies those States which may be liable for damage caused by a space object and which would have to pay compensation in such a case,

Taking note of the report of the Committee on the Peaceful Uses of Outer Space on its forty-second session[19] and the report of the Legal Subcommittee on its forty-first session, in particular the conclusions of the Working Group on the agenda item entitled "Review of the concept of the 'launching State'" annexed to the report of the Legal Subcommittee,[20]

Noting that nothing in the conclusions of the Working Group or in the present resolution constitutes an authoritative interpretation of or a proposed amendment to the Registration Convention or the Liability Convention,

Noting also that changes in space activities since the Liability Convention and the Registration Convention entered into force include the continuous development of new technologies, an increase in the number of States carrying out space activities, an increase in international cooperation in the peaceful uses of outer space and an increase in space activities carried out by non-governmental entities, including activities carried out jointly by government agencies and non-governmental entities, as well as partnerships formed by non-governmental entities from one or more countries,

---

[19]*Official Records of the General Assembly, Fifty-fourth Session, Supplement No. 20* and corrigendum (A/54/20 and Corr.l).

[20]A/AC.105/787, annex IV, appendix.

Desirous of facilitating adherence to and the application of the provisions of the United Nations treaties on outer space, in particular the Liability Convention and the Registration Convention,

1. *Recommends* that States conducting space activities, in fulfilling their international obligations under the United Nations treaties on outer space, in particular the Treaty on Principles Governing the Activities of States in the Exploration and Use of Outer Space, including the Moon and Other Celestial Bodies,[1] the Convention on International Liability for Damage Caused by Space Objects[3] and the Convention on Registration of Objects Launched into Outer Space,[4] as well as other relevant international agreements, consider enacting and implementing national laws authorizing and providing for continuing supervision of the activities in outer space of non-governmental entities under their jurisdiction;

2. *Also recommends* that States consider the conclusion of agreements in accordance with the Liability Convention with respect to joint launches or cooperation programmes;

3. *Further recommends* that the Committee on the Peaceful Uses of Outer Space invite Member States to submit information on a voluntary basis on their current practices regarding on-orbit transfer of ownership of space objects;

4. *Recommends* that States consider, on the basis of that information, the possibility of harmonizing such practices as appropriate with a view to increasing the consistency of national space legislation with international law;

5. *Requests* the Committee on the Peaceful Uses of Outer Space, in making full use of the functions and resources of the Secretariat, to continue to provide States, at their request, with relevant information and assistance in developing national space laws based on the relevant treaties.

D. Resolution 62/101 of 17 December 2007

Recommendations on enhancing the practice of States and international intergovernmental organizations in registering space objects

The General Assembly,

Recalling the Treaty on Principles Governing the Activities of States in the Exploration and Use of Outer Space, including the Moon and Other Celestial Bodies[1] (Outer Space Treaty), in particular articles VIII and XI,

Recalling also the Convention on Registration of Objects Launched into Outer Space,[4]

Recalling further its resolution 1721 B (XVI) of 20 December 1961,

Recalling its resolution 41/66 of 3 December 1986,

Taking note of the relevant parts of the report of the Committee on the Peaceful Uses of Outer Space on its fiftieth session[21] and the report of the Legal Subcommittee on its forty-sixth session, in particular the conclusions of the Working Group on the Practice of States and International Organizations in Registering Space Objects, annexed to the report of the Legal Subcommittee,[22]

Noting that nothing in the conclusions of the Working Group or in the present resolution constitutes an authoritative interpretation of or a proposed amendment to the Registration Convention,

Bearing in mind the benefits for States of becoming parties to the Registration Convention and that, by acceding to, implementing and observing the provisions of the Registration Convention, States:

(a) Enhance the utility of the Register of Objects Launched into Outer Space established under article III of the Registration Convention, in which information furnished by States and international intergovernmental

[21]*Official Records of the General Assembly, Sixty-second Session, Supplement No. 20* (A/62/20), paras. 209-215.

[22]See A/AC.105/891, annex III, appendix.

organizations conducting space activities that have declared their acceptance of the rights and obligations under the Registration Convention is recorded;

(b) Benefit from additional means and procedures that assist in the identification of space objects, including, in particular, in accordance with article VI of the Registration Convention,

Noting that States parties to the Registration Convention and international intergovernmental organizations conducting space activities, having declared their acceptance of the rights and obligations under the Convention, shall furnish information to the Secretary-General in accordance with the Convention and shall establish an appropriate registry and inform the Secretary-General of the establishment of such a registry in accordance with the Convention,

Considering that universal accession to and acceptance, implementation and observance of the provisions of the Registration Convention:

(a) Lead to increased establishment of appropriate registries;

(b) Contribute to the development of procedures and mechanisms for the maintenance of appropriate registries and the provision of information to the Register of Objects Launched into Outer Space;

(c) Contribute to common procedures, at the national and international levels, for registering space objects with the Register;

(d) Contribute to uniformity with regard to the information to be furnished and recorded in the Register concerning space objects listed in the appropriate registries;

(e) Contribute to the receipt of and recording in the Register of additional information concerning space objects on the appropriate registries and information on objects that are no longer in Earth orbit,

Noting that changes in space activities since the Registration Convention entered into force include the continuous development of new technologies, an increase in the number of States carrying out space activities, an increase in international cooperation in the peaceful uses of outer space and an increase in activities carried out by non-governmental entities, as well as partnerships formed by non-governmental entities from more than one country,

Desirous of achieving the most complete registration of space objects,

Desirous also of enhancing adherence to the Registration Convention,

1. *Recommends*, with regard to adherence to the Registration Convention,[4] that:

(a) States that have not yet ratified or acceded to the Registration Convention should become parties to it in accordance with their domestic law and, until they become parties, furnish information in accordance with General Assembly resolution 1721 B (XVI);

(b) International intergovernmental organizations conducting space activities that have not yet declared their acceptance of the rights and obligations under the Registration Convention should do so in accordance with article VII of the Convention;

2. *Also recommends,* with regard to the harmonization of practices, that:

(a) Consideration should be given to achieving uniformity in the type of information to be provided to the Secretary-General on the registration of space objects, and such information could include, inter alia:

(i) The Committee on Space Research international designator, where appropriate;

(ii) Coordinated Universal Time as the time reference for the date of launch;

(iii) Kilometres, minutes and degrees as the standard units for basic orbital parameters;

(iv) Any useful information relating to the function of the space object in addition to the general function requested by the Registration Convention;

(b) Consideration should be given to the furnishing of additional appropriate information to the Secretary-General on the following areas:

(i) The geostationary orbit location, where appropriate;

(ii) Any change of status in operations (inter alia, when a space object is no longer functional);

(iii) The approximate date of decay or re-entry, if States are capable of verifying that information;

(iv) The date and physical conditions of moving a space object to a disposal orbit;

(v) Web links to official information on space objects;

(c) States conducting space activities and international intergovernmental organizations that have declared their acceptance of the rights and obligations under the Registration Convention should, when they have designated focal points for their appropriate registries, provide the Office for Outer Space Affairs of the Secretariat with the contact details of those focal points;

3. *Further recommends,* in order to achieve the most complete registration of space objects, that:

(a) Due to the complexity of the responsibility structure in international intergovernmental organizations conducting space activities, a solution should be sought in cases where an international intergovernmental organization conducting space activities has not yet declared its acceptance of the rights and obligations under the Registration Convention, and a general backup solution should be provided for registration by international intergovernmental organizations conducting space activities in cases where there is no consensus on registration among the States members of such organizations;

(b) The State from whose territory or facility a space object has been launched should, in the absence of prior agreement, contact States or international intergovernmental organizations that could qualify as "launching States" to jointly determine which State or entity should register the space object;

(c) In cases of joint launches of space objects, each space object should be registered separately and, without prejudice to the rights and obligations of States, space objects should be included, in accordance with international law, including the relevant United Nations treaties on outer space, in the appropriate registry of the State responsible for the operation of the space object under article VI of the Outer Space Treaty;[1]

(d) States should encourage launch service providers under their jurisdiction to advise the owner and/or operator of the space object to address the appropriate States on the registration of that space object;

4. *Recommends* that, following the change in supervision of a space object in orbit:

(a) The State of registry, in cooperation with the appropriate State according to article VI of the Outer Space Treaty, could furnish to the Secretary-General additional information, such as:

- (i) The date of change in supervision;
- (ii) The identification of the new owner or operator;
- (iii) Any change of orbital position;
- (iv) Any change of function of the space object;

(b) If there is no State of registry, the appropriate State according to article VI of the Outer Space Treaty could furnish the above information to the Secretary-General;

5. *Requests* the Office for Outer Space Affairs:

(a) To make available to all States and international intergovernmental organizations a model registration form reflecting the information to be provided to the Office for Outer Space Affairs, to assist them in their submission of registration information;

(*b*) To make public, through its website, the contact details of the focal points;

(*c*) To establish web links on its website to the appropriate registries that are available on the Internet;

6. *Recommends* that States and international intergovernmental organizations should report to the Office for Outer Space Affairs on new developments relating to their practice in registering space objects.

E. Resolution 68/74 of 11 December 2013

Recommendations on national legislation relevant to the peaceful exploration and use of outer space

The General Assembly,

Emphasizing the importance of appropriate means of ensuring that outer space is used for peaceful purposes and that the obligations under international law and those specifically contained in the United Nations treaties on outer space[23] are implemented,

Recalling its resolutions 59/115 of 10 December 2004 on the application of the concept of the "launching State" and 62/101 of 17 December 2007 on recommendations on enhancing the practice of States and international intergovernmental organizations in registering space objects,

Taking note of the work of the Legal Subcommittee of the Committee on the Peaceful Uses of Outer Space and the report of its Working Group on National Legislation Relevant to the Peaceful Exploration and Use of Outer Space on the work conducted under its multi-year workplan,[24]

Noting that nothing in the conclusions of the Working Group or in the present recommendations constitutes an authoritative interpretation or a proposed amendment to the United Nations treaties on outer space,

Observing that, in view of the increasing participation of non-governmental entities in space activities, appropriate action at the national level is needed, in particular with respect to the authorization and supervision of non-governmental space activities,

---

[23]Treaty on Principles Governing the Activities of States in the Exploration and Use of Outer Space, including the Moon and Other Celestial Bodies (United Nations, *Treaty Series,* vol. 610, No. 8843); Agreement on the Rescue of Astronauts, the Return of Astronauts and the Return of Objects Launched into Outer Space (United Nations, *Treaty Series,* vol. 672, No. 9574); Convention on International Liability for Damage Caused by Space Objects (United Nations, *Treaty Series,* vol. 961, No. 13810); Convention on Registration of Objects Launched into Outer Space (United Nations, *Treaty Series,* vol. 1023, No. 15020); and Agreement Governing the Activities of States on the Moon and Other Celestial Bodies (United Nations, *Treaty Series,* vol. 1363, No. 23002).

[24]A/AC.105/C.2/101.

Noting the need to maintain the sustainable use of outer space, in particular by mitigating space debris, and to ensure the safety of space activities and minimize the potential harm to the environment,

Recalling the provisions contained in the United Nations treaties on outer space with respect to providing information, to the greatest extent feasible and practicable, on the activities carried out in outer space, in particular through registration of objects launched into outer space,

Noting the need for consistency and predictability with regard to the authorization and supervision of space activities and the need for a practical regulatory system for the involvement of non-governmental entities to provide further incentives for enacting regulatory frameworks at the national level, and noting that some States also include national space activities of a governmental character within that framework,

Recognizing the different approaches taken by States in dealing with various aspects of national space activities, namely by means of unified acts or a combination of national legal instruments, and noting that States have adapted their national legal frameworks according to their specific needs and practical considerations and that national legal requirements depend to a high degree on the range of space activities conducted and the level of involvement of non-governmental entities,

Recommends the following elements for consideration, as appropriate, by States when enacting regulatory frameworks for national space activities, in accordance with their national law, taking into account their specific needs and requirements:

1. The scope of space activities targeted by national regulatory frameworks may include, as appropriate, the launch of objects into and their return from outer space, the operation of a launch or re-entry site and the operation and control of space objects in orbit; other issues for consideration may include the design and manufacture of spacecraft, the application of space science and technology, and exploration activities and research;

2. The State, taking into account its obligations as a launching State and as a State responsible for national activities in outer space under the United Nations treaties on outer space, should ascertain national jurisdiction over space activities carried out from territory under its jurisdiction and/or control; likewise, it should issue authorizations for and ensure supervision over space activities carried out elsewhere by its citizens and/or legal persons established, registered or seated in territory under its jurisdiction and/or control, provided, however, that if another State is exercising jurisdiction with respect to such activities, the State should consider forbearing from duplicative requirements and avoid unnecessary burdens;

3. Space activities should require authorization by a competent national authority; such authority or authorities, as well as the conditions and procedures for granting, modifying, suspending and revoking the authorization, should be set out clearly within the regulatory framework; States might employ specific procedures for the licensing and/or for the authorization of different kinds of space activities;

4. The conditions for authorization should be consistent with the international obligations of States, in particular under the United Nations treaties on outer space, and with other relevant instruments, and may reflect the national security and foreign policy interests of States; the conditions for authorization should help to ascertain that space activities are carried out in a safe manner and to minimize risks to persons, the environment or property and that those activities do not lead to harmful interference with other space activities; such conditions could also relate to the experience, expertise and technical qualifications of the applicant and could include safety and technical standards that are in line, in particular, with the Space Debris Mitigation Guidelines of the Committee on the Peaceful Uses of Outer Space;[25]

5. Appropriate procedures should ensure continuing supervision and monitoring of authorized space activities by applying, for example, a system of on-site inspections or a more general reporting requirement; enforcement mechanisms could include administrative measures, such as the suspension or revocation of the authorization, and/or penalties, as appropriate;

6. A national registry of objects launched into outer space should be maintained by an appropriate national authority; operators or owners of space objects for which the State is considered to be the launching State or the State responsible for national activities in outer space under the United Nations treaties on outer space should be requested to submit information to the authority to enable the State on whose registry such objects are carried to submit the relevant information to the Secretary-General of the United Nations in accordance with applicable international instruments, including the Convention on Registration of Objects Launched into Outer Space,[4] and in consideration of General Assembly resolutions 1721 B (XVI) of 20 December 1961 and 62/101 of 17 December 2007; the State may also request information on any change in the main characteristics of space objects, in particular when they have become non-functional;

7. States could consider ways of seeking recourse from operators or owners of space objects if their liability for damage under the United Nations

[25] *Official Records of the General Assembly, Sixty-second Session, Supplement No. 20* (A/62/20), annex.

treaties on outer space has become engaged; in order to ensure appropriate coverage for damage claims, States could introduce insurance requirements and indemnification procedures, as appropriate;

8. Continuing supervision of the space activities of non-governmental entities should be ensured in the event of the transfer of ownership or control of a space object in orbit; national regulations may provide for authorization requirements with regard to the transfer of ownership or obligations for the submission of information on the change in status of the operation of a space object in orbit.

Part four

Other documents

A. Space Debris Mitigation Guidelines of the Committee on the Peaceful Uses of Outer Space[26]

1. Background

Since the Committee on the Peaceful Uses of Outer Space published its Technical Report on Space Debris in 1999,[27] it has been a common understanding that the current space debris environment poses a risk to spacecraft in Earth orbit. For the purpose of this document, space debris is defined as all man-made objects, including fragments and elements thereof, in Earth orbit or re-entering the atmosphere, that are non-functional. As the population of debris continues to grow, the probability of collisions that could lead to potential damage will consequently increase. In addition, there is also the risk of damage on the ground, if debris survives Earth's atmospheric re-entry. The prompt implementation of appropriate debris mitigation measures is therefore considered a prudent and necessary step towards preserving the outer space environment for future generations.

Historically, the primary sources of space debris in Earth orbits have been *(a)* accidental and intentional break-ups which produce long-lived debris and *(b)* debris released intentionally during the operation of launch vehicle orbital stages and spacecraft. In the future, fragments generated by collisions are expected to be a significant source of space debris.

Space debris mitigation measures can be divided into two broad categories: those that curtail the generation of potentially harmful space debris in the near term and those that limit their generation over the longer term. The former involves the curtailment of the production of mission-related space debris and the avoidance of break-ups. The latter concerns end-of-life procedures that remove decommissioned spacecraft and launch vehicle orbital stages from regions populated by operational spacecraft.

---

[26]Endorsed by the Committee on the Peaceful Uses of Outer Space at its fiftieth session and contained in A/62/20, annex, and endorsed by the General Assembly in its resolution 62/217 of 22 December 2007.

[27]United Nations publication, Sales No. E.99.I.17.

2. Rationale

The implementation of space debris mitigation measures is recommended since some space debris has the potential to damage spacecraft, leading to loss of mission, or loss of life in the case of manned spacecraft. For manned flight orbits, space debris mitigation measures are highly relevant due to crew safety implications.

A set of mitigation guidelines has been developed by the Inter-Agency Space Debris Coordination Committee (IADC), reflecting the fundamental mitigation elements of a series of existing practices, standards, codes and handbooks developed by a number of national and international organizations. The Committee on the Peaceful Uses of Outer Space acknowledges the benefit of a set of high-level qualitative guidelines, having wider acceptance among the global space community. The Working Group on Space Debris was therefore established (by the Scientific and Technical Subcommittee of the Committee) to develop a set of recommended guidelines based on the technical content and the basic definitions of the IADC space debris mitigation guidelines, and taking into consideration the United Nations treaties and principles on outer space.

3. Application

Member States and international organizations should voluntarily take measures, through national mechanisms or through their own applicable mechanisms, to ensure that these guidelines are implemented, to the greatest extent feasible, through space debris mitigation practices and procedures.

These guidelines are applicable to mission planning and the operation of newly designed spacecraft and orbital stages and, if possible, to existing ones. They are not legally binding under international law.

It is also recognized that exceptions to the implementation of individual guidelines or elements thereof may be justified, for example, by the provisions of the United Nations treaties and principles on outer space.

4. Space debris mitigation guidelines

The following guidelines should be considered for the mission planning, design, manufacture and operational (launch, mission and disposal) phases of spacecraft and launch vehicle orbital stages:

Guideline 1: Limit debris released during normal operations

Space systems should be designed not to release debris during normal operations. If this is not feasible, the effect of any release of debris on the outer space environment should be minimized.

During the early decades of the space age, launch vehicle and spacecraft designers permitted the intentional release of numerous mission-related objects into Earth orbit, including, among other things, sensor covers, separation mechanisms and deployment articles. Dedicated design efforts, prompted by the recognition of the threat posed by such objects, have proved effective in reducing this source of space debris.

Guideline 2: Minimize the potential for break-ups during operational phases

Spacecraft and launch vehicle orbital stages should be designed to avoid failure modes which may lead to accidental break-ups. In cases where a condition leading to such a failure is detected, disposal and passivation measures should be planned and executed to avoid break-ups.

Historically, some break-ups have been caused by space system malfunctions, such as catastrophic failures of propulsion and power systems. By incorporating potential break-up scenarios in failure mode analysis, the probability of these catastrophic events can be reduced.

Guideline 3: Limit the probability of accidental collision in orbit

In developing the design and mission profile of spacecraft and launch vehicle stages, the probability of accidental collision with known objects during the system's launch phase and orbital lifetime should be estimated and limited. If available orbital data indicate a potential collision, adjustment of the launch time or an on-orbit avoidance manoeuvre should be considered.

Some accidental collisions have already been identified. Numerous studies indicate that, as the number and mass of space debris increase, the primary source of new space debris is likely to be from collisions. Collision avoidance procedures have already been adopted by some Member States and international organizations.

Guideline 4: Avoid intentional destruction and other harmful activities

Recognizing that an increased risk of collision could pose a threat to space operations, the intentional destruction of any on-orbit spacecraft and launch vehicle orbital stages or other harmful activities that generate long-lived debris should be avoided.

When intentional break-ups are necessary, they should be conducted at sufficiently low altitudes to limit the orbital lifetime of resulting fragments.

Guideline 5: Minimize potential for post-mission break-ups resulting from stored energy

In order to limit the risk to other spacecraft and launch vehicle orbital stages from accidental break-ups, all on-board sources of stored energy should be depleted or made safe when they are no longer required for mission operations or post mission disposal.

By far the largest percentage of the catalogued space debris population originated from the fragmentation of spacecraft and launch vehicle orbital stages. The majority of those break-ups were unintentional, many arising from the abandonment of spacecraft and launch vehicle orbital stages with significant amounts of stored energy. The most effective mitigation measures have been the passivation of spacecraft and launch vehicle orbital stages at the end of their mission. Passivation requires the removal of all forms of stored energy, including residual propellants and compressed fluids and the discharge of electrical storage devices.

Guideline 6: Limit the long-term presence of spacecraft and launch vehicle orbital stages in the low-Earth orbit (LEO) region after the end of their mission

Spacecraft and launch vehicle orbital stages that have terminated their operational phases in orbits that pass through the LEO region should be removed from orbit in a controlled fashion. If this is not possible, they should be disposed of in orbits that avoid their long-term presence in the LEO region.

When making determinations regarding potential solutions for removing objects from LEO, due consideration should be given to ensuring that debris that survives to reach the surface of the Earth does not pose an undue risk to people or property, including through environmental pollution caused by hazardous substances.

Guideline 7: Limit the long-term interference of spacecraft and launch vehicle orbital stages with the geosynchronous Earth orbit (GEO) region after the end of their mission

Spacecraft and launch vehicle orbital stages that have terminated their operational phases in orbits that pass through the GEO region should be left in orbits that avoid their long-term interference with the GEO region.

For space objects in or near the GEO region, the potential for future collisions can be reduced by leaving objects at the end of their mission in an orbit above the GEO region such that they will not interfere with, or return to, the GEO region.

5. Updates

Research by Member States and international organizations in the area of space debris should continue in a spirit of international cooperation to maximize the benefits of space debris mitigation initiatives. This document will be reviewed and may be revised, as warranted, in the light of new findings.

6. Reference

The reference version of the IADC space debris mitigation guidelines at the time of the publication of this document is contained in the annex to document A/AC.105/C.1/L.260.

For more in-depth descriptions and recommendations pertaining to space debris mitigation measures, Member States and international organizations may refer to the latest version of the IADC space debris mitigation guidelines and other supporting documents, which can be found on the IADC website (www.iadconline.org).

B. Safety Framework for Nuclear Power Source Applications in Outer Space[28]

Preface

Nuclear power sources (NPS) for use in outer space have been developed and used in space applications where unique mission requirements and constraints on electrical power and thermal management precluded the use of non-nuclear power sources. Such missions have included interplanetary missions to the outer limits of the Solar System, for which solar panels were not suitable as a source of electrical power because of the long duration of these missions at great distances from the Sun.

According to current knowledge and capabilities, space NPS are the only viable energy option to power some space missions and significantly enhance others. Several ongoing and foreseeable missions would not be possible without the use of space NPS. Past, present and foreseeable space NPS applications include radioisotope power systems (for example, radioisotope thermoelectric generators and radioisotope heater units) and nuclear reactor systems for power and propulsion. The presence of radioactive materials or nuclear fuels in space NPS and their consequent potential for harm to people and the environment in Earth's biosphere due to an accident require that safety should always be an inherent part of the design and application of space NPS.

NPS applications in outer space have unique safety considerations compared with terrestrial applications. Unlike many terrestrial nuclear applications, space applications tend to be used infrequently and their requirements can vary significantly depending upon the specific mission. Mission launch and outer space operational requirements impose size, mass and other space environment limitations not present for many terrestrial nuclear facilities. For some applications, space NPS must operate autonomously at great distances from Earth in harsh environments. Potential accident conditions resulting from launch failures and inadvertent re-entry could expose NPS to extreme physical conditions. These and other unique safety considerations for the use of space NPS are

[28]Endorsed by the Committee on the Peaceful Uses of Outer Space at its fifty-second session and contained in A/AC.105/934.

significantly different from those for terrestrial nuclear systems and are not addressed in safety guidance for terrestrial nuclear applications.

After a period of initial discussion and preparation, the Scientific and Technical Subcommittee of the Committee on the Peaceful Uses of Outer Space of the United Nations and the International Atomic Energy Agency (IAEA) agreed in 2007 to jointly draft a safety framework for NPS applications in outer space. This partnership integrated the expertise of the Scientific and Technical Subcommittee in the use of space NPS with the well-established procedures of IAEA for developing safety standards pertaining to nuclear safety of terrestrial applications. The Safety Framework for Nuclear Power Source Applications in Outer Space represents a technical consensus of both bodies.

The Safety Framework is intended to be utilized as a guide for national purposes. As such, it provides voluntary guidance and is not legally binding under international law.

The Safety Framework is not a publication in the IAEA Safety Standards Series, but it is intended to complement the Safety Standards Series by providing high-level guidance that addresses unique nuclear safety considerations for relevant launch, operation and end-of-service mission phases of space NPS applications. It complements existing national and international safety guidance and standards pertaining to terrestrial activities that involve the design, manufacture, testing and transportation of space NPS. The Safety Framework has been developed with due consideration of relevant principles and treaties. The Safety Framework does not supplement, alter or interpret any of those principles or treaties.

The focus of the Safety Framework is the protection of people and the environment in Earth's biosphere from potential hazards associated with relevant launch, operation and end-of-service mission phases of space NPS applications. The protection of humans in space is an area of ongoing research and is beyond the scope of the Safety Framework. Similarly, the protection of environments of other celestial bodies remains beyond the scope of the Safety Framework.

Safety terms used in the Safety Framework are defined in the IAEA Safety Glossary. As used herein, the term "nuclear safety" includes radiation safety and radiation protection. Additional terms specific to space NPS applications are defined in the section of the Safety Framework entitled "Glossary of terms".

In summary, the purpose of the Safety Framework is to promote the safety of NPS applications in outer space; as such, it applies to all space NPS applications without prejudice.

The Scientific and Technical Subcommittee and IAEA wish to express their appreciation to all those who assisted in the drafting and review of the text of the Safety Framework and in the process of reaching consensus.

Introduction

Background

Nuclear power sources (NPS) for use in outer space[29] have been developed and used on spacecraft where unique mission requirements and constraints on electrical power and thermal management precluded the use of non-nuclear power sources. Such missions have included interplanetary missions to the outer limits of the Solar System, for which solar panels were not suitable as a source of electrical power because of the long duration of the mission at great distances from the Sun.

Past, present and foreseeable space NPS applications include radioisotope power systems (including radioisotope thermoelectric generators and radioisotope heater units) and nuclear reactor systems for power and propulsion. Space NPS have enabled several ongoing missions. According to current knowledge and capabilities, space NPS are the only viable energy option to power some foreseeable space missions and significantly enhance others.

Both normal operating and potential accident conditions for space NPS applications, through the launch, operation and end-of-service phases, are radically different from the conditions for terrestrial applications. The launch and outer space environments create very different safety design and operational criteria for space NPS. Furthermore, space mission requirements lead to unique mission-specific designs for space NPS, spacecraft, launch systems and mission operations.

The presence of radioactive materials or nuclear fuels in space NPS and their consequent potential for harm to people and the environment in Earth's biosphere due to an accident require that safety must always be an inherent part of the design and application of space NPS. Safety (i.e. protection of people and the environment)[30] should focus on the entire application and not only on the space NPS component. All elements of the application could affect the nuclear aspects of safety. Therefore, safety needs to be addressed in the context of the entire space NPS application, which includes the space NPS, spacecraft, launch system, mission design and flight rules.

[29]As used herein, the term "outer space" is synonymous with "space".

[30]As used herein, the term "people and the environment" is synonymous with the term "people and the environment in Earth's biosphere".

Purpose

The purpose of this publication is to provide high-level guidance in the form of a model safety framework. The framework provides a foundation for the development of national and international intergovernmental safety frameworks while allowing for flexibility in adapting such frameworks to specific space NPS applications and organizational structures. Such national and international intergovernmental frameworks should include both technical and programmatic elements to mitigate risks arising from the use of space NPS. Implementation of such frameworks not only would provide assurance to the global public that space NPS applications would be launched and used in a safe manner, but could also facilitate bilateral and multilateral cooperation on space missions using NPS. The guidance provided herein reflects an international consensus on measures needed to achieve safety and applies to all space NPS applications without prejudice.

Scope

The Safety Framework for Nuclear Power Source Applications in Outer Space focuses on safety for relevant launch, operation and end-of-service phases of space NPS applications. High-level guidance is provided for both the programmatic and technical aspects of safety, including the design and application of space NPS. However, detailed usage of this guidance depends on the particular design and application. Implementation of the guidance provided in the Safety Framework would supplement existing standards that cover other aspects of space NPS applications. For example, activities occurring during the terrestrial phase of space NPS applications, such as development, testing, manufacturing, handling and transportation, are addressed in national and international standards relating to terrestrial nuclear installations and activities. Similarly, non-nuclear safety aspects of space NPS applications are addressed in relevant safety standards of governments and international intergovernmental organizations (e.g. regional space agencies).

A substantial body of knowledge exists for establishing a space NPS application safety framework for people and the environment in Earth's biosphere. However, comparable scientific data do not yet exist that would provide a technically sound basis for developing a space NPS application framework for protecting humans in the unique conditions in space and beyond Earth's biosphere. Therefore, the protection in space of humans involved in missions that use space NPS applications is beyond the scope of the Safety Framework. Similarly, the protection of environments of other celestial bodies remains beyond the scope of the Safety Framework.

Safety objective

The fundamental safety objective is to protect people and the environment in Earth's biosphere from potential hazards associated with relevant launch, operation and end-of-service phases of space nuclear power source applications.

Governments, international intergovernmental organizations and non-governmental entities that are involved in space NPS applications should take measures to ensure that people (individually and collectively) and the environment are protected without unduly limiting the uses of space NPS applications.

Guidance for satisfying the fundamental safety objective is grouped into three categories: guidance for governments (section 3 below) applies to governments and relevant international intergovernmental organizations that authorize, approve or conduct space NPS missions; guidance for management (section 4 below) applies to the management of the organization that conducts space NPS missions; and technical guidance (section 5 below) applies to the design, development and mission phases of space NPS applications.

Guidance for governments

This section provides guidance for governments and relevant international intergovernmental organizations (e.g. regional space agencies) that authorize, approve or conduct space NPS missions. Governmental responsibilities include establishing safety policies, requirements and processes; ensuring compliance with those policies, requirements and processes; ensuring that there is acceptable justification for using a space NPS when weighed against other alternatives; establishing a formal mission launch authorization process; and preparing for and responding to emergencies. For multinational or multiorganizational missions, governing instruments should define clearly the allocation of these responsibilities.

Safety policies, requirements and processes

Governments that authorize or approve space nuclear power source missions should establish safety policies, requirements and processes.

Governments and relevant international intergovernmental organizations that authorize or approve space NPS missions, whether such missions are conducted by governmental agencies or by non-governmental entities, should establish and ensure compliance with their respective safety policies, requirements and processes to satisfy the fundamental safety objective and fulfil their safety requirements.

Justification for space nuclear power source applications

The government's mission approval process should verify that the rationale for using the space nuclear power source application has been appropriately justified.

Space NPS applications may introduce risk to people and the environment. For this reason, governments and relevant international intergovernmental organizations that authorize, approve or conduct space NPS missions should ensure that the rationale for each space NPS application considers alternatives and is appropriately justified. The process should consider benefits and risks to people and the environment related to relevant launch, operation and end-of-service phases of the space NPS application.

Mission launch authorization

A mission launch authorization process for space nuclear power source applications should be established and sustained.

The government that oversees and authorizes the launch operations for space NPS missions should establish a mission launch authorization process focused on nuclear safety aspects. The process should include an evaluation of all relevant information and considerations from other participating organizations. The mission launch authorization process should supplement the authorization processes covering non nuclear and terrestrial aspects of launch safety. An independent safety evaluation (i.e. a review, independent of the management organization conducting the mission, of the adequacy and validity of the safety case) should be an integral part of the authorization process. The independent safety evaluation should consider the entire space NPS application—including the space NPS, spacecraft, launch system, mission design and flight rules—in assessing the risk to people and the environment from relevant launch, operation and end-of-service phases of the space mission.

Emergency preparedness and response

Preparations should be made to respond to potential emergencies involving a space nuclear power source.

Governments and relevant international intergovernmental organizations that authorize, approve or conduct space NPS missions should be prepared to respond rapidly to launch and mission emergencies that may result in radiation exposure of people and radioactive contamination of Earth's environment. Emergency preparedness activities include emergency planning, training, rehearsals and development of procedures and communication protocols, including the drafting of potential accident notifications. Emergency response plans should be designed so as to restrict radioactive contamination and radiation exposure.

Guidance for management

This section provides guidance for management of the organizations involved in space NPS applications. In the context of the Safety Framework, management should comply with governmental and relevant intergovernmental safety policies, requirements and processes to satisfy the fundamental safety objective. Management responsibilities include accepting prime responsibility for safety, ensuring the availability of adequate resources for safety and promoting and sustaining a robust safety culture at all organizational levels.

Responsibility for safety

The prime responsibility for safety should rest with the organization that conducts the space nuclear power source mission.

The organization that conducts the space NPS mission has the prime responsibility for safety. That organization should include, or have formal arrangements with, all relevant participants in the mission (spacecraft provider, launch vehicle provider, NPS provider, launch site provider etc.) for satisfying the safety requirements established for the space NPS application.

Specific safety responsibilities for management should include the following:

(a) Establishing and maintaining the necessary technical competencies;

(b) Providing adequate training and information to all relevant participants;

(c) Establishing procedures to promote safety under all reasonably foreseeable conditions;

(d) Developing specific safety requirements, as appropriate, for missions that use space NPS;

(e) Performing and documenting safety tests and analyses as input to the governmental mission launch authorization process;

(f) Considering credible opposing views on safety matters;

(g) Providing relevant, accurate and timely information to the public.

Leadership and management for safety

Effective leadership and management for safety should be established and sustained in the organization that conducts the space nuclear power source mission.

Leadership in safety matters should be demonstrated at the highest levels in the organization that conducts the mission. Management of safety should be integrated with the overall management of the mission. Management should develop, implement and maintain a safety culture that ensures safety and satisfies the requirements of the governmental mission launch authorization process.

The safety culture should include the following:

(a) Clear lines of authority, responsibility and communication;

(b) Active feedback and continuous improvement;

(c) Individual and collective commitment to safety at all organizational levels;

(d) Safety accountability of the organization and of individuals at all levels;

(e) A questioning and learning attitude to discourage complacency with regard to safety.

Technical guidance

This section provides technical guidance for organizations involved in space NPS applications. This guidance is pertinent to the design, development and mission phases of space NPS applications. It encompasses the following key areas for developing and providing the technical basis for the authorization and approval processes and for emergency preparedness and response:

(a) Establishing and maintaining a nuclear safety design, test and analysis capability;

(b) Applying that capability in the design, qualification and mission launch authorization processes of the space NPS application (i.e. space NPS, spacecraft, launch system, mission design and flight rules);

(c) Assessing the radiation risks to people and the environment arising from potential accidents and ensuring that the risk is acceptable and as low as reasonably achievable;

(d) Taking action to manage the consequences of potential accidents.

Technical competence in nuclear safety

Technical competence in nuclear safety should be established and maintained for space nuclear power source applications.

Having technical competence in nuclear safety is vital for satisfying the safety objective. From the earliest point in the development of a space NPS application, organizations should establish, consistent with their responsibilities, nuclear safety design, test and analysis capabilities, including qualified individuals and facilities, as appropriate. Those capabilities should be maintained for the duration of the relevant phases of the space NPS missions.

Competence in nuclear safety should include:

(a) Defining space NPS application accident scenarios and their estimated probabilities in a rigorous manner;

(b) Characterizing the physical conditions to which the space NPS and its components could be exposed in normal operations, as well as potential accidents;

(c) Assessing the potential consequences to people and the environment from potential accidents;

(d) Identifying and assessing inherent and engineered safety features to reduce the risk of potential accidents to people and the environment.

Safety in design and development

Design and development processes should provide the highest level of safety that can reasonably be achieved.

The underlying approach to satisfying the safety objective should be to reduce the risks from normal operations and potential accidents to as low a level as is reasonably achievable by establishing comprehensive design and development processes that integrate safety considerations in the context of the entire space NPS application (i.e. space NPS, spacecraft, launch system, mission design and flight rules). Nuclear safety should be considered from the earliest stages of design and development and throughout all mission phases. The design and development processes should include:

(a) Identifying, evaluating and implementing design features, controls and preventive measures that:

- (i) Reduce the probability of potential accidents that could release radioactive material;
- (ii) Reduce the magnitude of potential releases and their potential consequences;

(b) Incorporating lessons learned from prior experience;

(c) Verifying and validating design safety features and controls through tests and analyses, as appropriate;

(d) Using risk analysis to assess the effectiveness of design features and controls and to provide feedback to the design process;

(e) Using design reviews to provide assurance of the safety of the design.

Risk assessments

Risk assessments should be conducted to characterize the radiation risks to people and the environment.

The radiation risks to people and the environment from potential accidents during relevant launch, operation and end-of-service phases of space NPS applications should be assessed and uncertainties quantified to the extent possible. Risk assessments are essential for the mission launch authorization process.

Accident consequence mitigation

All practical efforts should be made to mitigate the consequences of potential accidents.

As part of the safety process for space NPS applications, measures should be evaluated to mitigate the consequences of accidents with the potential to release radioactive material into Earth's environment. The necessary capabilities should be established and made available, as appropriate, for timely support of activities to mitigate the consequences of accidents, including:

(a) Developing and implementing contingency plans to interrupt accident sequences that could lead to radiation hazards;

(b) Determining whether a release of radioactive material has occurred;

(c) Characterizing the location and nature of the release of radioactive material;

(d) Characterizing the areas contaminated by radioactive materials;

(e) Recommending protective measures to limit exposure of population groups in the affected areas;

(f) Preparing relevant information regarding the accident for dissemination to the appropriate governments, international organizations and non-governmental entities and to the general public.

Glossary of terms

The glossary below defines terms that are specific to space NPS applications. General safety terms used in the Safety Framework are defined in the *IAEA Safety Glossary, 2007 Edition.*[31]

End-of-service phase: the period of time after the useful life of a spacecraft

Flight rules: a collection of pre-planned decisions to minimize the amount of real-time decision-making required for nominal and off-nominal situations affecting a mission

Launch: a set of actions at the launch site leading to the delivery of a spacecraft to a predetermined orbit or flight trajectory

Launch phase: the period of time that includes the following: pre-launch preparation at the launch site, lift-off, ascent, operation of upper (or boost) stages, payload deployment and any other action associated with delivery of a spacecraft to a predetermined orbit or flight trajectory

Launch vehicle: any propulsive vehicle including upper (or boost) stages constructed for placing a payload into space

Launch system: the launch vehicle, launch site infrastructure, supporting facilities, equipment and procedures required for launching a payload into space

Mission: launch and operation (including end-of-service aspects) of a payload (e.g. spacecraft) beyond Earth's biosphere for a specific purpose

Mission approval: permission by a governmental authority for activities to proceed for preparing a mission for launch and operation

Mission design: the design of a space mission's trajectory and manoeuvres based on mission objectives, launch vehicle and spacecraft capabilities and mission constraints

Mission launch authorization: permission by a governmental authority to launch and operate a mission

Space nuclear power source: a device that uses radioisotopes or a nuclear reactor for electrical power generation, heating or propulsion in a space application

Space nuclear power source application: the overall system (space nuclear power source, spacecraft, launch system, mission design, flight rules etc.) involved in conducting a space mission involving a space nuclear power source.

---

[31]International Atomic Energy Agency, *IAEA Safety Glossary: Terminology Used in Nuclear Safety and Radiation Protection, 2007 Edition* (Vienna, 2007).